PRAISE FOR *SWEET + SALTY*

"Anyone who has struggled with living ethically while giving space for daily pleasures will find a kindred spirit in Lagusta Yearwood, an self-proclaimed 'fake back-to-the-land anarcho-punk' whose love for chocolate and fellow creatures, human and non-human, is infectious from page 1 of this book. Her vulnerability and openness infuse the book's tone throughout, making you trust her hard-won expertise in the delicate art of vegan chocolate confectionary-making. As your guide, Yearwood is uncommonly kind, humble, and generous, and we're so lucky to have all been invited into her shop."

—SOLEIL HO, restaurant critic of *The San Francisco Chronicle*

"Any journey upstate must include a visit to Lagusta's sweet shops, and her highly personalized, beautiful book is captures this experience perfectly."

—TERRY H. ROMERO, author of *Show Up for Salad* and coauthor of *Veganomicon*

Caramel Apples (page 111)

Harissa Truffles (page 62)

sweet + salty

The Art *of* Vegan Chocolates, Truffles,

Caramels, and More *from* Lagusta's Luscious

LAGUSTA YEARWOOD

Foreword *by* BROOKS HEADLEY
James Beard Award Winner

LIFE
LONG

Da Capo Lifelong Books
Hachette Book Group
1290 Avenue of the Americas, New York, NY 10104
www.dacapopress.com
@DaCapoPress

Printed in the United States of America

First Edition: September 2019

Published by Da Capo Lifelong Books, an imprint of Perseus Books, LLC, a subsidiary of Hachette Book Group, Inc. The Da Capo Lifelong Books name and logo is a trademark of the Hachette Book Group.

The Hachette Speakers Bureau provides a wide range of authors for speaking events. To find out more, go to www.hachettespeakersbureau.com or call (866) 376-6591.

The publisher is not responsible for websites (or their content) that are not owned by the publisher.

Print book interior design by Tabitha Lahr
Library of Congress Cataloging-in-Publication Data has been applied for.

ISBNs: 978-0-7382-3507-3 (hardcover); 978-0-7382-3506-6 (ebook)

LSC-C

10 9 8 7 6 5 4 3 2 1

To the best one
Pauline Dubkin Yearwood

—•—•—•—•—•—

And also

To

Kathryn Elizabeth Vrooman Larson

The kindest, the softest.

I am amazed by your actual human self every day.

—•—•—•—•—•—

And also

To

The Lagusta's Luscious,

Commissary! &

Confectionery!

crews & customers

Earl Grey and Preserved Orange Bars (page 199)

contents

foreword

Have you ever wondered why chocolate costs two dollars? It starts as a bean, right? A bean that gets extracted from a pod and then fermented somewhere near the equator and then processed into, say, a Whatchamacallit or a Toffifay or a Dove bar and sold near the POS system at a deli on the Upper West Side or a 7-Eleven in Alhambra or Tokyo? Why is it so cheap? Why is it so sweet? Does it hurt your teeth?

Have you ever been to Confectionery!, a, well, ahem, confectionery shop in the East Village of Manhattan? Have you noticed that it always smells really good? Like good flowers and chocolate fumes and some kind of weird nonhippie incense that must cost a bundle to source? If someone were to wander into this shop at 440 East Ninth Street, would they be able to get a chocolate bar for two bucks?

Have you ever been to a superfancy restaurant? The kind that cost five hundred bucks for dinner and culminate in a flurry of chocolate bonbons of all different colors, angular and bulbous shapes and flavors that typically creep into an amorphous blob of *cocoa-adjacent* after three bites? Do you even want to shotgun a bunch of thinly coated ganache after a grand buffet of lobster, truffles, and foie gras?

Now, the chocolate *confections* at Confectionery!, are they on par with the toniest of black-tie, hospitality-included, Michelin plaque–decorated restaurants? Would you think I am nuts if I tell you they are better? That the flavors are more focused and crystallized? That the shells are more lithe? That despite the fact that the ganache filling of, say, one of Lagusta's tahini meltaways is completely void of dairy, vegan as all get out, it rivals and tackles the creaminess of a heavy cream–addicted chocolatier in Dallas or midtown? And these candies, while being outrageously interesting and craveable, and made entirely with coconut milk as the "dairy," don't taste a drop like coconut? How is that possible? Is Lagusta an alchemist, holed up in the woods of New Paltz, and shuttling down bonbons to sell to the socialites and aging hard-core kids of New York City who may or may not even be vegan themselves? Are the candies just that good?

Why does Lagusta's chocolate cost a little more (sometimes a lot more) than those 100

Grands and Reese's at eye level at a Wegmans checkout? Is it because she sources ethically sound chocolate base material, stuff that isn't ambiguously draped in slavery and oppression? In 2019, is it still revolutionary to say *you don't have to fuck people over to survive*? Is a ten-dollar chocolate bar a luxury item? Or the right price for the right thing when made right?

Somewhere within the self-congratulatory world of high-end food cookery, is there a lobotomizing machine that the sous chefs and pastry assistants and chefs de cuisine must hook up with probes to their skulls to make sure that exactly 0.0 percent thought is put into using raw materials that do not shred the environment and the folks and animals that live in it?

Do you want to learn how Lagusta Yearwood pulls this shit off? Let's read, man.

—**Brooks Headley** owner/operator
Superiority Burger

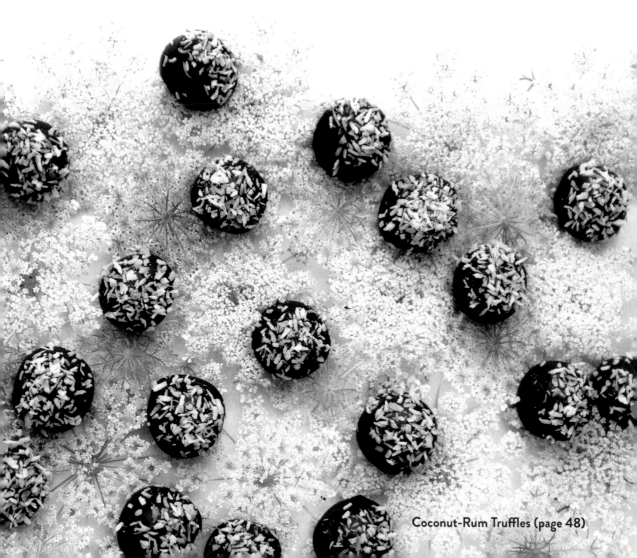

Coconut-Rum Truffles (page 48)

introduction:

are you there, sugar? it's me, lagusta

As a kid, I wanted the weird candies no one likes: those buttercream mints that melt cloyingly in your mouth, watermelon bubble gum, anything with sour flavors. Chocolate seemed stupid. I'd eat a Snickers for the caramel and nougat, or a Butterfinger for the peanut butter, but mostly I wanted the clean hit of pure sugar.

Technically, we didn't eat sugar in our household, because my mom was a hippie who embraced every countercultural value she could get her hands on. I grew up in Phoenix because my parents' Volkswagen van broke down on the drive to California. Most Phoenicians have similar origin stories. My parents joined a community of burnouts who couldn't quite get it together to make it to the hippie promised land, but my mother wasn't a burnout (my dad is another story). She was a journalist who worked as a theater critic most of my childhood. She could never bring herself to enforce any rules or discipline—it didn't square with her antiauthoritarian nature. Plus, she was busy working. So, we ate our sweets in semisecret.

We always had chopped-up raw vegetables around, carrots and green bell peppers and sprouts, and some hummus or cottage cheese. Ritz crackers. Peanut butter. My mom, kicking off her mom-pumps and dingy soft bra and exhaustedly changing into a faded tie-dyed sundress after work, mostly said we could "graze" for dinner, halfheartedly positing it as a treat—have whatever you want! We barely ate meat at home, just hot dogs when we had cookouts a few times a year. Our skimpy, overgrazed fridge sometimes had not much more in it than a jar of rancid wheat germ, margarine, a few foraged oranges from a tree down the street, and limpid celery. Ants on a log was an entire food group. When things felt fancy, we replaced the peanut butter with slicks of cream cheese, unwrapping the foil-wrapped brick lovingly.

I have no memories of anyone ever making dessert. Our birthday cakes, the glorious exception to all rules, were always supermarket ones with fat puffy roses, lurid food coloring staining shortening frosting–scalloped edges. We shoved our face into them and emerged baptized in fluorescent frosting, vibrating with the twinned happinesses of a birthday and sugar overload. We guarded the mounds of frosting decorations like snapping wolves, wouldn't let anyone eat the corner pieces, fantasized about flavors the rest of the year.

Mostly, we ate junk from the liquor store on the corner of our block. My dad sent us there a lot with permission slips to buy beer. This was Arizona in the 1980s and '90s and no one had any problem with this system. My brother and I would lug home a sixer of whatever was cheapest with fifty cents' worth of candy balanced on top, a Snickers bar or Hydrox cookie mini pack, watermelon Bubble Yum or, my favorite, de la Rosa, a peanut marzipan round packaged in a cellophane wrapper with a delicate rose printed on it. De la Rosa is a perfect confection. Just crumbly enough, just sweet enough. Megasimple. Gorgeously packaged. My mouth is watering right now.

I ate homemade food and dessert, sort of, at my dad's mom's place, a doublewide trailer in a trailer park with a swimming pool half an hour from our house. My grandmother had grown up desperately poor, and the world of packaged food was a constant source of joy and revelation to her—her pantry was stocked layers deep with store-brand cans, boxes, packets. She kept a coffee can filled with bacon drippings on the counter at all times. Lots of squishy white bread my mom warned us against as if it was Chernobyl waste.

My grandmother was a giddy, fun-loving, alcoholic racist who called me Gusta with the hardest *g* you've ever heard. She got DUIs in her pickup truck until her driver's license was taken away, but she didn't mind—she just made

Jimmy drive her to the St. Vincent de Paul thrift stores instead of driving herself. She could never believe her luck at having found, after five tries, a husband who didn't beat her up. Jimmy worked as truck driver in a mine that dynamited the mountains that encircled Phoenix. His wardrobe consisted only of Hanes white T-shirts and Levi's. He came home at night and amiably drank twelve or fifteen Budweisers until he gently passed out. When I announced my newfound vegetarianism to him, he softly said, "Wheeeeeeeeellllllll," drawing it out for an impressively long time.

My grandmother subscribed to a lot of magazines. *Sunset, Woman's Day, Redbook*. My mother and I pored over *Taste of Home*, joyfully mocking the down-home, Midwestern aw-shucks aesthetic, with perforated recipes to clip, columns for recipe exchange requests, "My Mom's Best Meal," and "Country Kitchen Tours"—full-color spreads of beaming housewives showing off their collection of hen-themed salt shakers and pot holders. My ultrafeminist, nondomestic mom shook her head at the seeming anti-intellectualism and family obsession, so I did, too. But the recipes fascinated me. It would have never occurred to me to make any of them. They seemed like strange equations that it wasn't my place to solve. It was my first exposure to food writing.

I got heavily into animal rights when I was fifteen. When I got deeper into the animal rights world, my mom joined me, going to meetings and giving up meat herself. Phoenix wasn't a liberal town then or now, and the tiny animal rights scene was close-knit and fierce. Within a few months of going to meetings, I knew I had to go vegan. So we did it, my mom and me. We mail-ordered lip gloss from the PETA catalog. We'd drive to the health food store in Tempe, forty-five minutes away, to get tofu (what did we do with the tofu? I'm afraid to remember). We slipped up a few times, but then I kept a mental picture of suffering cows from John Robbins's classic *Diet for a New America* (the dude was heir to the Baskin Robbins fortune and went vegan! I love this book still). I'd call up whenever I wanted a Snickers. And just like that, I was vegan.

By the time I was seventeen, I was president of Arizona's biggest animal rights group—though technically my mom was copresident because the bylaws said the president had to be at least eighteen. By then, we were both vegan. Everyone deep into the animal rights world was. You couldn't be a serious activist and eat dairy, and all I really wanted was to be a serious activist.

When I met my ex-partner, Jacob, my freshman year in college in 1997, his appetite for edible treats of all kinds was already deep and, at times, all-consuming. For two decades, we celebrated everything big and small with sweets: grocery-store sorbet eaten from the pint on the floor of the house we just closed on; lavish cakes made by our best friend Maresa to toast our anniversary; hand-pounded mochi made at the Buddhist temple down the street to celebrate the New Year; an endless parade of birthday cakes at restaurants, at friend's houses, at home with just the two of us snuggled up together, spooning up good wishes for the year to come.

After college, I went to culinary school because I wanted to learn to make vegan food as decadent and sophisticated and transformative as the best "regular" food available. I wanted to show that not eating animal products was an ethical choice, and that vegans can care about—and be as knowledgeable about, and as wildly passionate about—food just as much as any meat-eating

modern chef trying to cook from a personal point of view. We're all trying to tell a story through food. Mine is of decadence and indulgence, of the best flavors and seeing how far I can push them. It's also about still trying to live as an activist, to use my job as a way to advance my ethics.

After culinary school, I started working as a private chef around Manhattan. "Private cheffing" is a lucrative slash soul-crushing business. Once, during an initial meeting with a new client, I asked whether her kitchen was stocked with such basics as olive oil and salt and pepper. She airily said she thought so, sure, probably—well, go take a look? I walked into a completely bare room and opened the refrigerator to reveal fifty or sixty bottles of nail polish, a rainbow of soldiers lined up neatly in the door compartments. "That's a twenty-year collection, honey!" the woman yelled after me. I made her the same salad for six months in a row, a daikon and steamed shiitake thing with apple cider vinegar that she'd read was slimming.

At one point, I started just cooking out of my house and delivering to my clients. Like all my businesses, this meal delivery service—which would become my full-time job for the next nine years—was born with no business plan, capital, savings, investors, health department permit, or business sense. The only thing I had was a desire not to work for someone else and the endless energy of someone terrified about not being able to pay next month's rent. It was enough! That skittish, panicked energy propelled me through practically a decade of fifteen-hour days. In time, I rented a commercial kitchen and worked my way through John Waters's catalog, obsessively watching and rewatching *Female Trouble* while chopping 40 or 50 pounds of onions at a time in one small room with twelve gas burners bubbling away at all times. The meal delivery taught me how to cook.

Meanwhile, in 2003, Jacob and I made some vegan truffles as Christmas and Hanukkah gifts for our friends and families. I ripped off a truffle recipe from *Martha Stewart Living* and subbed soy creamer (so processed! It was a different era. I was a different Lagusta.) for the cream and coconut oil for the butter. Everyone loved them, so I started making them on my days off, taking orders among my friends and family and eventually setting up a primitive website for them. Soon, I was shipping hastily packaged boxes of truffles across the country every week. It would take me another five years or so of gleefully shipping chocolates that would arrive in horrifying condition to refine my chocolate-shipping techniques. Amazingly, we still have customers from those days.

Our shipping operation is still laughably small—just two tables crammed with repurposed cornstarch packing peanuts (mostly given to us by our local health food store—none of us can pop in for some dried mango or scallions without leaving with a car full of air pillows and packing peanuts), endless rolls of "quiet tape" (Always Splurge on the Quiet Tape: a cardinal Lagusta's Luscious rule reinforced every time we have to endure the strangely ear-splitting screech of cheapie packing tape), compostable ribbon (it costs more than gold but it's not made with toxic dyes—plus our ribbon guy, Ken, is a riot on the phone), tissue paper, compostable ice packs we buy by the pallet, and custom shipping boxes (printed right in New Paltz!).

All that came later. By 2010, I was exhausted by the weekly marathon of organizing customers for the meal delivery service, grocery shopping, cooking the food-mountain, washing the mountain of containers, then piping, rolling, dipping, packaging, and shipping a few hundred truffles on my "days off."

Wary of giving up my sacred John Waters-watching solitude but knowing I needed help, I'd hired two sous chefs: Veronica and Maresa. (Today, over ten years later, Maresa is my best friend and business partner and Veronica runs the New York City shop that Maresa and I co-own. Employee retention is my finest accomplishment, by far.)

When I opened the door to interview Veronica—the first person I ever interviewed—I knew immediately that she was perfect. I still chase that feeling in interviews: does it feel as it felt when I first met Veronica, or Rachel, or Kate? Hiring people is a sort of falling in love (later on, I did fall in real-deal, true-blue love with Kate, but that's a story for another book, ah).

Veronica was seventeen but said she was eighteen. She had just shaved off a Technicolor Mohawk. She didn't and still doesn't know how to drive, so her parents drove her forty-five minutes to my dinky yellow kitchen every week and sat in the car, reading, for eight hours. Veronica can tell you anything you want to know about early Dylan, Van Morrison, Japanese avant-garde/modernist poetry, Leonard Cohen, what films are currently at Film Forum, what exhibits are worthwhile at literally every art museum in Manhattan (the free admission days of which she has planned her days off around). Veronica skews heavily Luddite when it comes to computers and social media. Veronica was homeschooled, can you tell?

I'd met Maresa at the Rosendale farmers' market, using the immutable law of the universe known as Two Vegans Converging on a Small Space in a Small Town at the Same Time Every Week Will Eventually Become Best Friends. She was selling produce for her neighbor and cupcakes she'd made. Every week, I bought a cupcake, and eventually we started talking, then she started showing up at my kitchen. I said I didn't need to hire someone (I did; I was just scared to be a boss to two people at once), so she said she would work for free. She worked for free one day, and that night, I offered her a full-time job. She and I worked long days together every day for the next six years until I fired her so she could work full-time at her own baking business, conveniently located in the back room of the Lagusta's Luscious production space, where she rents a postage stamp–size mini-kitchen and works literally around the clock with a tiny crew of fiercely devoted bakers just as intensely focused as she is. In 2016, we opened a joint sweets shop in New York City, Confectionery! with her French macarons and baked goods and Lagusta's Luscious's confections.

Kate

Back in the yellow kitchen, once Vern and Reesey were trained ("Stop stirring so much! Let it get a little browned."—there, you've taught someone how to cook.), I gently slid into a slow-motion overwork-induced nervous breakdown that had been building for a decade. Things weren't quite as fiscally tenuous with the business, so I allowed myself to realize how exhausted I was. During this period, I mostly sat in my car parked in front of the kitchen, paralyzed with deep-burn exhaustion, dreading hauling the hundreds of pounds of produce inside, sharpening the knives, beginning the cycle again.

The deeper I went in the food world, the more I thought about chocolate. With Jacob's

Rachel

Veronica

Maresa

chocolate-loving palate at my side, we'd begun tasting the new breed of craft chocolate that had been springing up. It took me a while to taste anything but bitter flavors, but in time my taste buds opened up, and a chocolate bar became a box to unpack: a dozen or so flavors gradually unfolding on my tongue.

When new people start at the shop and they can't taste the port in the Port-Walnut Truffle or whether the Corn Bar has enough corn, I'm always annoyingly on them to keep tasting, keep tasting, keep tasting. It sounds kind of like a joke when you first start, but your job depends on your knowing these flavors. Recipes are, to a certain extent, junk. Too many variables. Your tongue has to be the final say. The only real difference between food professionals and everyone else is crazy amounts of tasting, and trying to learn a little more every time. I love when someone realizes they know exactly how the Corn Bar should taste, and that without a little more smoked salt, it's crap.

Gradually, I learned what I liked and didn't: sour flavors in chocolate itself were out (my tongue belongs to sour candies for life, but sour chocolate, ugh), which cut out some prominent American bean-to-bar makers. Super-high-percentage (read: bitter) chocolate with a big honking sour/dry/astringent nose turns me off immediately. Bean-to-bar makers are so proud of using fewer and fewer ingredients in their bars, but chocolate bars made from just cacao beans that maybe for a second glanced at a bag of sugar, with no vanilla or luxurious emulsifiers like soy lecithin let into the building at all, feel unbalanced and goopy in my mouth. Not like a treat. I felt like a failure in the world of hipster 90% chocolate until one day I realized: **who cares?** There's plenty of chocolate out there. I kept tasting and making truffles. I started making caramels and toffees and brittles and bonbons. I still love candy more than chocolate.

In December 2010, Jacob and I drove to our friend Conor's wedding at the Cloisters in upper Manhattan. On the drive, I was whining about not wanting to cook so much every week and Jacob said, "What about if you opened a chocolate shop?" So, I did. I was thirty-two and had been working two full-time jobs for ten years. Running a small chocolate shop sounded like a dream.

Until 2016, whatever I happened to be doing at the time for money was named Lagusta's Luscious: private cooking in someone's home, making chocolates, savory food, whatever. I regret the name. I figured I'd be a one-woman show, and having employees work for such a ludicrously named business makes me feel sheepish. But my friend Noel, who I met working at Bloodroot, a feminist collective restaurant in Connecticut, named the business, and when I see it through her (fierce 1970s dyke-style) eyes I love it: a deceptively cute name for a high-minded, very personal cottage industry.

Lagusta's Luscious, chocolate shop version, opened on Jacob's birthday, June 28, 2011. Maresa and I were the only employees. We didn't plan on opening a shop, exactly. We put in a counter and two metal metro shelves for bars and barks and bonbons, but we didn't really talk about customer service, or how we were going to handle helping customers while producing product. It was surprising to us that customers came. In retrospect, that seems strange. We were selling chocolate. In a small town. With no other fine chocolate options. Where we'd built up our reputation as chefs and confectioners for years. People came.

Alexis

Jenn

Erika

Jenna

When we opened, we had trouble keeping fifty or seventy-five pieces of chocolate in the display case (now we have a few hundred in the case at a time and about a thousand in reserve, impatiently waiting their turn). We'd regularly hand customers truffles that had been dipped in chocolate about three seconds beforehand. We made to order everything for our website orders: if we got an order for one box of pomegranate truffles, we made eight pomegranate truffles, put them in a box, and walked that box to the post office. We were always late, always rushing, always understocked, never had any money, always took on more than we could handle. Maresa regularly banged on the post office door at 5:05 p.m. until they accepted her armload of packages (this trick has never worked for me. On the other hand, I've never tried it. Maresa is from a large Italian family from Staten Island and gets away with lots of things—from earrings to semolina bread procurement—that I'd never have the guts to attempt. She's my best friend and I'm still scared of her. Once, I asked her whether she was popular in high school, because I'd vowed that I would never be friends with anyone who was popular in high school. She stared at me. I stared at her. "Wait," I said. "You were a bully in high school, weren't you?" She stared at me. "I didn't let anyone push me around, if that's what you're asking," she said, and went back to weighing out sugar).

Our hugely inefficient working style is laughable to think about now, but I know our current systems and production methods are still small-batch and home-style when compared with other chocolatiers. It doesn't bother me. The more efficient we get the bigger we get, and I don't want to get much bigger. Plus, the business has built-in inefficiencies because of our commitment to unfashionable concepts, such as collective decision-making and obsessively scrutinazing our supply chain. But I like running it this way, and it's more fun, and why do we have to keep growing, anyway?

I've identified as an anarchist as long as I can remember. Not the bomb-throwing kind (yep, there's another kind!), the kind who believes that the goal of being human is to own one's destiny, not to put it in the care of the capitalist state. Anarchism is about power: who has it and who doesn't. I wanted to keep all of my own power and renounce power over all others. I started working for myself because I wanted to own my life. When I started realizing that apparently "owning my life" now meant hiring a bunch of people and (as I saw it in my bad times) owning their lives, too, I had no idea how to function. My core belief was that no one should be forced to let a dumb top-down hierarchal structure determine their life, they should be allowed to live wildly according to their own plan.

In retrospect, I was bonkers. It took me about four years to come around, though. I'm a slow learner. I wasn't a very good boss during those years. If I can provide good jobs to my community, I owe it to my employees to stop being wishy-washy about being their boss and just learn how to be good at it. So, I have (been trying).

I use two principles informed by anarchism daily in the business: (1) the starting point of any decision should be informed by more than just capitalist principles; and (2) organization without repression, which is to say: we can run efficiently and well without oppressing those around us. (Of course, we're attempting to use a by-definition weakened form of anarchism within the framework of a completely wrecked capitalist world order. But still, why not try?)

By the fall of 2014, things were going great. I'd made my peace with being a boss. We were gearing up for the holiday season. I was figuring out how to make Drinking Chocolate Magic Spheres when my mother called me. Magic Spheres are hollow chocolate balls with marshmallows trapped inside. To make Drinking Chocolate Magic Spheres, you put the spheres in a mug and pour hot milk (of vegan variety) over them and whisk and magic: a hot chocolate with marshmallows is born. Except that getting the technique to make the spheres right was taking endless practice. (All magic, culinary or otherwise, has a recipe behind it that took hours or days or months or years to perfect.) I didn't pick up my phone when my mom called because I had chocolate all over my hands. A little while later I listened to the message. Her voice was faux-light. I could tell right away it was bad. My mom and I were never mother and daughter. We were always best friends. When I was a kid and she used to say that, it annoyed me, because I wanted and needed a mom and that wasn't her strong suit. But once I was an adult, our closeness was the most important relationship in my life.

On November 13, 2014, my mother was diagnosed with terminal pancreatic cancer. In December, I moved her from Chicago to be with me. I took the next year pretty much completely off from work. I'd spent fifteen years building a career for myself: obsessing over every detail, micromanaging every recipe, staying late at work every night, missing vacations and holidays and birthday parties because I was too focused on putting in my time. On November 12, 2014, I didn't think the shop could function without me for a day. By the next November, the shop had been functioning pretty much completely without me for a year. I ran my business through texts and e-mails and phone calls from doctor's offices and hospitals and rehab facilities and moving cars while everyone else made chocolates and helped customers and planned seasonal specials and shipped packages and ordered inventory. The shop closed in on itself, gently: a self-regulating, self-functioning unit. It was shocking how little they needed me.

I threw myself into caretaking, and of course it was the most intense experience of my life. Getting to spend so much time with my mom, who had lived halfway across the country from me for eighteen years, was amazing. We'd sneak into the chocolate shop after driving back upstate from chemo and gorge on ice cream and Matzo Toffee. We had picnics under magnolia trees and long conversations in the car about the finer points of contemporary animal rights theory and practice. My mom became the chocolate shop mascot, hanging out on the couch in the break area when I could shimmy in some work time. She told our mostly vegan crew stories of animal rights protests she'd been on, she gossiped about customers, everyone saved her the crispiest bits of Maple Honeycomb before it was enrobed, made her coffee with scoops of ice cream in it, and gave their recommendations for the best weed-infused foods to eat postchemo. My mom was a hippie who never gave up a love of youth culture, so hanging out with a bunch of cool women in their early twenties was a dream. Whenever anyone mentioned a band, no matter how obscure, no matter if they only played in punk basements in New Paltz, she always said the same thing, "Oh yeah...I've heard of them. I think..."

When the caretaking really ramped up, around June, and I needed extra help, Kate and Maresa and Jacob took care of me. And when I needed even more help, it turned out that in the ten years I'd spent living in New Paltz, I'd quietly created a fierce community around me. Customers and friends were constantly checking in on me, offering rides, running errands, bringing meals. Farmer friends brought endless bags of homegrown produce so I could cook good meals for my mom. Weed dealers brought medicinal marijuana tinctures and butters. My solitary introvert heart softened and kept softening. I spent 2015 watching my best friend die, and it felt exactly that hard. But at times it felt like the best year, too. I spent every day with my best friend. And I leaned into the help that was offered, for the first time in my scrappy sole proprietorship life.

Christmas week 2015 was the busiest week the chocolate shop had ever had. I didn't work at all in December. We set up home hospice care for my mom in early December and I sat in my mother's apartment two blocks from the shop for thirteen days without leaving. I sat by her bed and watched *Seinfeld* and read Carson McCullers and Flannery O'Connor while squirting morphine and red wine into her mouth in ever-increasing quantities. At night Kate or Jacob or Maresa or all three came home from working at my job and told me the gossip and brought me food. My mom had stopped eating at that point. They rubbed my shoulders or my mom's feet or held me while I cried. One night my mom said she wanted to have mimosas, so I made it a party. I texted everyone who worked at the shop and invited them over, asking them to bring champagne or seltzer or orange juice, and we gathered around my mom's bed and toasted her. Everyone hung out for a long time and we gossiped like we gossip at the shop, bringing the shop to her: will the patriarchy-fighting effects of selfie culture save us all? Can misandrists love drag queens? Will the new Thai restaurant in town have vegan options? She gurgled with happiness at all these cool kids surrounding her.

A few days before Christmas, I woke up from a few hours of sleep and she wasn't there anymore. Her last words were, "Today is going to be a really fun day!"

A good strategy for dealing with grief and coming out of the hardest year of your life is to take some time off for relaxation and reflection.

Instead, within four months, I'd opened two more businesses.

I was adrift in every way. Orphaned and suddenly bereft of the major responsibility of the past year, I dazedly returned to work at the chocolate shop to the odd realization that I was superfluous. The year without me had made everyone so good at their jobs all I needed to do was float around, tasting chocolates for quality control, overseeing things, pitching in when a holiday came around.

I could have taken this new freedom, the first I'd ever had in my working life, as a chance to do things like have days off or be at home long enough in the mornings for my hair to dry before stuffing it into a work-approved scarf. But I hate a vacuum.

In February, friends mentioned that their gallery space right off Main Street was going up for rent. Jacob and I had offhandedly talked about opening a café there where I could make savory food again and Jacob could indulge a coffee fixation. Then, Maresa and I decided to open up a small retail joint sweets shop in New York City. These things go like these things go, and one week in March I signed two leases: one on East Ninth street in the East Village, and one on Church Street in New Paltz. We opened both shops within two weeks of each other in May, and now I've folded myself in thirds, a letter addressed to Work, and spend my days running between the café, Commissary!—the chocolate shop two blocks away, and Confectionery!—our sweets shop a cool two hours south.

I've never gone back to making chocolates daily. The chocolate shop is a self-regulating organism, a tight crew that works more efficiently than I'd have thought possible. I'm water, I flow where there's a drought. More and more I see myself as a business owner instead of a chocolatier. I'm not suited to interacting with so many people every day, but the challenge of running this three-headed Hydra in a way in line with my weirdo lefty anarchist values keeps me racing to work every day with wet hair. I used to think it was shameful to want to do well. But now I want to do well because I want to pay my employees better—what's shameful about that? Food businesses make money by saving on labor, overhead, or food costs. Without skimping in horrifying ways in one arena, you can't really make it. But what if I can? While using local fruit grown by friends down the road, while paying good wages to people who love their jobs and work hard every day, while packaging everything in ways that don't make us feel sick when we think of the waste? What if we were somehow miraculously allowed to live good lives? What if we squeak through the system?

◆ • ◆ • ◆

Black (or Red) Raspberry–Lime Truffles (page 35)

bitter: ethical issues in chocolate and sugar production

a.k.a.: Our Piddling Attempt to Sleep at Night

ᄭᄭᄭᄭᄭᄭᄭᄭᄭᄭᄭᄭᄭᄭᄭᄭᄭᄭᄭᄭᄭᄭᄭᄭᄭᄭᄭᄭᄭᄭᄭᄭᄭᄭᄭᄭᄭᄭ

CHOCOLATE

Okay. Let's just say it. A lot of chocolate is made with questionable labor practices, including human trafficking and the use of child slaves to harvest cacao pods. No one disputes this—not Hershey, not Mars, not Nestlé. These huge manufacturers (the "big three" chocolate giants) have taken steps to curb the worst human rights abuses in the chocolate industry, but at a sickeningly slow pace.

I got into the chocolate business because I wanted to find a pleasurable way to live my activist values: fairness, equality, and compassion. It's why I'm vegan, and it's why our shop uses only fairly produced chocolate.

I knew that there were ethical minefields involved in chocolate production, but it wasn't until I read the exhaustively researched and meticulously reported book *Bitter Chocolate*, by Carol Off, that I realized how wide-ranging and horrifying the human rights abuses associated with African-produced chocolate are.

I read the book on vacation at the beach in Hawaii after a wildly busy holiday season. Every minute for the past two months had been spent making ganache, dipping caramels, packing boxes, shipping out boxes. We were all texting all our friends, begging them to come in for an hour or five to wrap bars or tie ribbons or wash dishes. I finally flew to Hawaii on Christmas Day and collapsed on the beach.

I figured that *Bitter Chocolate* would be illuminating as a refresher on the issues I already knew to exist (and circumnavigated by using fair trade chocolate). But the chapters about the corruption and dilution of the fair trade label convinced me that simply using fair trade chocolate isn't enough to ensure slave-free chocolate.

My chocolate consumption patterns changed after *Bitter Chocolate*. My entire business model was based on ethical chocolate. I had to go deeper. I stopped buying even fair trade chocolate from West Africa. Now all of our chocolate comes from fair trade farms in Peru and Ecuador—but it's a fraught position for a chocolatier, cutting out Africa entirely: what about the producers who truly are building an ethical chocolate culture in West Africa? I hope someday soon I'll have the guts to seek them out and support their work. The nature of capitalism is that it flattens discourse, and right now the word is that ethical chocolate from West Africa is an impossibility. Our business specializes in strange concepts we have to constantly explain to customers—high-end vegan chocolates with a focus on savory flavors, an X-rated chocolate named for a body part no one wants to say (Furious Vulvas!), supersmall seasonal batches that mean your favorite flavor might be gone next week, social media captions that border on nonsensical—when customers come in and ask whether we use African chocolate because they've heard it's bad, those are the ethical, caring customers we want. Educating my staff to explain one more thing to them, with the high probability that they'll walk away because West African chocolate = bad chocolate, is a risky business. In time, though, I have goals.

With all this in mind, here are some ideas for how to cut your risk of buying chocolate that would make you sick if you heard how the cacao beans it's made from were harvested.

With some exceptions (overpriced terrible chocolate is definitely a thing), you do get what you pay for with chocolate: higher-end pricier chocolate is (usually) more likely to be made with beans that don't participate in the forced-labor system. Buying fair trade chocolate is a good starting point, even though, like most large and complex regulatory systems, it can be an imperfect system. If you're buying bulk chocolate from a larger company, buy fair trade.

But if you're splurging on a beautiful bar from a small-batch bean-to-bar chocolate maker (the big guys make chocolate from beans, too, so that's not a perfect descriptor, but you know what I mean: one of those new fancy places stocked with interestingly groomed people wearing very expensive aprons), chances are it was produced under okay ethical conditions—with a price tag to match. Most fancy-apron chocolate makers are proud of where their beans come from and often oversee their production themselves in a supertransparent process that goes far beyond the conditions covered under the fair trade label. Chocolate like this is made for eating, not recipes. For the recipes in this book, use a good-quality vegan chocolate from a medium-size company that puts ethics at the forefront of its sourcing practices, such as Republica del Cacao, Tcho, Theo, or Taza, or look for organic and fair trade bulk chocolate from a bigger maker, such as Valrhona, Callebaut, or Guittard.

The chocolate we use comes primarily from Peru, Ecuador, and the Dominican Republic, as well as Hawaii—where cacao farms are beginning to spring up in place of cheap hotels or luxury condos and would-be farmers are flocking to the islands to participate in the increasing chocolate economy. Hawaiian chocolate in bulk is profit-killingly pricey, but I swear it smells and tastes flowery, all plumeria undertones and a silky body that I love.

Chocolate can be grown all around the equator, and in the warming world we live in, can be a good crop to plant as part of a jungle-style ecosystem to green areas razed by monocropping or deforestation. Cacao is an understory tree that does best when planted alongside larger shade trees, making it a good component of a biodiverse farm.

The future of chocolate looks good. Small producers with big hearts are taking over more and more of a market share, and even large chocolate manufacturers are becoming more transparent about their sourcing practices and are realizing that in a more connected world, ethics matter more to everyone. As always, the reason companies care about these issues is because their customers do. Ask questions, contact companies. Feel good about what you're working with so intimately in the kitchen.

SUGAR

Unlike chocolate, no one really seems to care about how sugar gets to us. Spoiler: it's not pretty. Land grabs by massive sugar conglomerates that displace indigenous people, deforest and destroy already fragile ecosystems, and threaten habitat loss; excessive fertilizer usage that results in poisoned water and soils; working conditions that include child labor, massive inhumanities, and yep, forced labor. Sugar is one of the most sickeningly political agricultural products we come into daily contact with—and has been for hundreds of years. The history of sugar is fascinating and disgusting.

It's not a fashionable cause in activist circles today, but historically, sugar's horrific journey to teacups and dessert plates has been the locus of political activism spanning decades and continents.

Sugar obsession took hold in the 1500s and hasn't let up. Five centuries later and sugar production has literally changed the face of the planet: entire civilizations have been erased because of it, millions of people enslaved to produce it, countless acres of ecosystems destroyed for it, untold numbers of wildlife murdered for it through habitat destruction.

By the 1600s, the lust for sugar was so intense that a driving factor for the coming industrial revolution was demand for improved technology to build and run sugar mills. Similarly, one of the primary drivers of the New World slave trade was a need for workers in sugar plantations.

The modern idea of "human rights" came about in part as a response to the way workers on sugar plantations were treated. Abolitionists boycotted slave-grown sugar in the eighteenth century until slavery was abolished after a solid three hundred years of slave-produced sugar, but conditions on sugar plantations haven't improved as much as we'd like to believe in the centuries since. Today, most of our sugar is still harvested by people of color who aren't paid enough, work under almost unspeakably bleak conditions, and have little other job opportunities or are coerced into work. In the Dominican Republic, where a huge proportion of American sugar comes from, Haitian cane cutters are coerced to work long hours with little food, not enough water, no overtime pay, inadequate health care, and live in shacks without running water, electricity, or schools for their children, who often work in the cane fields before and after school.

The United States became the nation that it is partially because of power conferred by sugar profits: sugar money helped it win independence from Great Britain. A few centuries later, Big Sugar's political influence was such that Hawaii is a state because its sugar plantations were too valuable to be left alone by American industrialists, so an unlawful coup backed by US sugar barons deposed the Hawaiian queen.

It's all depressing, and obviously there aren't any easy answers.

But we're not going to stop eating sugar. So, the best system we've got is the fair trade and organic certification processes. The best sugars are fair trade and organic, but because pesticides aren't widely used on sugar cane, if you have to choose between organic sugar or fair trade sugar, the fair trade label is your best bet. It's not perfect, but looking for the fair trade logo is better than giving up entirely on the dream of an ethical supply chain, right?

At its worst (when forms are fudged, certifications are conferred through bribery, and standards aren't enforced), the fair trade process overlays a system of accountability to stem the worst horrors of modern sugar production. At its best, fair trade transforms the lives of sugar cane workers, ensuring that the people who produce a product we clearly don't want to live without are treated like human beings with intrinsic value.

"ETHICAL CONSUMPTION" HA HA HA

Why do we work with ingredients oozing such sickening backstories?

You probably know how it is: researching any product—coffee, cotton, sneakers—leads to a horrifying sinking sense that our lust for endless consumption at increasingly cheap prices has created an infinite loop of unfair labor practices and environmentally destructive production values.

Knowing that consumers are waking up to the sad side of capitalism, an increasing number of businesses of all sizes are creating boutique products with meticulous ethics that consumers can feel more comfortable about buying.

The phrase *ethical consumption* is pretty gross. The idea that we can buy ourselves out of the planetary destruction and labor exploitation created by American-style capitalism is pretty absurd. And most activists would tell you nothing will change until we smash the entire capitalist system. I'm sure they're mostly right. In the bigger picture, anyway. But I don't have twenty years to throw at the revolution, to devote to dismantling our destructive form of capitalism. I want a life that's fair—to my employees, to the farmers and workers making the products we use, to my customers and to myself—right now. So, I'm doing what I can within the confines of the society we're in to bring that about.

And also? I like it. I like my life. I love making my little business into an arrow toward a world I want to live in. I started out in life as an activist and I run my business with an activist heart. Surprisingly (or not), many of my former activist colleagues now run small businesses focusing on ethical consumption. You work underground in a slaughterhouse for a year, filming piglets being smashed to death and crying every night, and afterward you need to do something soft with your life that's still in line with your values, so as not to implode. So, my friend Liz, shell-shocked after doing just that, started roasting coffee. Now she imports fairly sourced beans and has become an expert roaster, quietly veganizing third-wave coffee spots who hire her as a consultant. My friend Tara was exhausted by an adolescence spent starting Gay/Straight Alliances and volunteering for Greenpeace and slowly shifted from principled idealism to principled realism, started cooking in restaurants, discovered anarchism, and now runs a punk skincare company making cruelty-free face oil, deodorants, and soaps. It's not the revolution; I'm not pretending it is. It's just a way to live a life you don't feel too gross about.

The rub is, of course, that because these nice thoughtful lovingly crafted products reflect a real price paid for raw materials and to those who created them, they're often accessible only to those with disposable income.

My little company lives right here. While I'm proud of our products, I'm not delusional: I know that systemic changes need to be made in our society to ensure that not only wealthy consumers have access to fairly made goods. We're working on one end of the spectrum to bring about societal changes that need to be made to be able to live in a more just and fair world, but there is much work to be done that is beyond the scope of our little chocolaty world at Lagusta's Luscious. A more egalitarian society, the society I hope I'm working for every day, needs people on all sides of the activist spectrum. We desperately need traditional activists working within the current system to bring about change, and we need feminists and idealists and nonviolent anarchists running businesses in feminist and idealist and anarchist ways, remaking our little universes according to our own values and refusing to compromise.

I intentionally started a business making conventionally nonvegan products that are traditionally made with wildly unethical ingredients. I intentionally market to nonvegans. Vegans eat vegan food every day. What I like is blowing peoples' minds with confections that don't "taste vegan."

What I really want is to be a Trojan horse. People are going to eat junk food. If I can make junk food that tastes as good as mainstream, conventional junk food but is made with lefty weirdo heart-on-sleevey radical politix—unfashionable ideas like fairness and equality and people not dying to harvest cacao beans or cut sugar cane—and if I can give some people in my community good jobs making fancy candy all day long—it seems like a decent way to live.

There are million ways we could be better. But we're trying, and my mission is to see where we're failing, and commit myself to always keeping my eyes open and trying to do better. We'll never be finished, but at least I feel like I'm on a path that feels right. At least I can sleep at night, and at least I get to eat some candy every day.

References:

Bitter Chocolate by Carol Off
Sugar: A Bittersweet History by Elizabeth Abbott
Fresh Fruit, Broken Bodies by Seth M. Holmes

otherwise known as sugar the great: a sweet shop lexicon

Chocolate words tend to be loosely defined. One shop's "bonbon" is another's "praline," which is another's "truffle." Every chocolatier works in a particular style based on their training, geography, and preference. And different regions and countries have different meanings for different terms.

Here is how we define things in our shop and in this book:

BAR: Chocolate bars are called chocolate bars because they're made in chocolate bar molds, or cut into chocolate bar shapes. They can be filled with caramel, ganache (which I can't resist calling "truffle bars" even though that breaks the hardline rule I lay down in the "truffles" section), smoked shiitake mushroom fudge, or anything else, or they can be solid and packed (or not) with nuts, herbs, seeds, or anything else (these additions are called, in chocolate parlance, "inclusions"), or they can be simply pure chocolate, à la the Hershey bar.

BARK: To my mind, the only thing that differentiates a bar from a bark is size. At our shop, we make a variety of barks in a bigger size than our bars because their flavors lend themselves to a bigger canvas, or because they just look prettier that way. See: Slate.

BONBON: A catchall term for all chocolates, particularly nontruffles. Not bon-bon, not bon bon, not pronounced all fancy Fronchy "bohn-bohn," just bonbon.

BRITTLE: Toffee minus fat plus more sugar—usually (peanut brittle, for example, sometimes has some fat). Brittles are quick and generally simple, and are most often made with nuts or seeds.

CARAMEL: Caramel candies are sugar plus fat plus time, but not too much time—otherwise you'll end up with toffee (or a really burnt pot). Caramels are generally soft and take their name from their glorious browned color. Most caramels in this book are medium-soft, because very soft caramels can be irksome to work with.

Caramel sauce is sugar plus (optional) fat plus time plus more fat thrown in at the end. But you can make a caramel candy into caramel sauce, oh yes you can. Just melt it down and thin it a little with water.

CREAM: Chocolates made with a thin chocolate shell filled with a cream made of fondant, white chocolate, impossibly rich nut pastes, or any kind of light-colored creamy fillings.

FONDANT: *Fondant* used to mean "a tasty and delightful candy made of mostly sugar." Somewhere along the line it came to mean "a very beautiful but very cardboardy-tasting edible sugar-dough sheet used to cover cakes." Guess which version we prefer.

GANACHE BONBON: This is a term I developed to name chocolates that are made of ganache but aren't truffles. Sometimes these are basically square truffles, which taste almost identical to round truffles (one could argue that some of the pleasure of the bite is diminished by the square corners, which don't fit the palate as perfectly) but are approximately one thousand times faster to make, so we can sell them a little cheaper. Sometimes these are molded chocolates, which are also infinitely quicker than truffles and can be made in a huge number of shapes. There's nothing wrong with ganache bonbons; I sometimes need to remind myself and my crew. They're just not truffles (which just might be the most special treats on the planet).

PRALINE: Here's where things get messy. In the American South, a praline (pronounced pra-leen)

is a sugary nutty candy puck made with pecans. In France and Belgium and Europe generally, praline or praliné (pronounced pra-lee-nay) refers to any chocolate made with praline paste (a mixture of caramelized sugar and nuts, usually almonds or hazelnuts). Basically, if something is labeled "praline," you can bet it's got some nuts in it.

SLATE: A slate is a very thin bark.

TOFFEE: Toffee is made of the same basic ingredients as caramel (fat, a type of milk, sugar, plus a syrup) but is cooked to a higher temperature than caramel and crunches rather than melts in your mouth. Unless it's humid, in which case—don't.

TRUFFLE: I'm kind of a stickler about this one. Truffles were named for truffle mushrooms, which are round and knobby and blobby and rough and carry a sense of the earth they were found in. To my (overly fussy) mind, a truffle is a round, handmade confection. Many sweet shops sell all kinds of chocolates as "truffles," and, well, the English language is a continually evolving living document, right? But I'll toe the line on this one. I love that chocolate truffles are named for truffle mushrooms. It reminds me not to take them too seriously, and to continue making them by hand, even late at night when my hands are tired from rolling and the pull of truffle molds that make identical perfect spheres is strong. Sometimes our boozy and fruity truffles leak a bit of their alcohol. We could fix this by using less alcohol or fruit, but then the flavor would suffer. Like a truffle mushroom, a chocolate truffle is about an explosion of intense flavor, not a perfect exterior.

Truffles are especially fun to make because they lend themselves to creative garnishing.

Molded chocolates need to be painted with cocoa butter paints to have a garnish (molded chocolates are made upside down, so the top of the chocolate is trapped inside the mold until the chocolate is dry and set), but truffles can be garnished as they are dipped in chocolate, one by one.

Because truffles are somewhat of a purist's chocolate, we tend to garnish ours with a purist's sensibility. Metonymy is our default principle—a little bit of the flavor of the truffle stands in as a metaphor for the truffle itself. Fennel–Apple Skin Truffles are garnished with a sprinkle of fennel pollen; Beet Coriander Truffles, with a bit of beet powder. These garnishes don't add much flavor, but contribute visual interest and speak to the earthy vernacular truffles seem most at home in.

That all sounded pretty pretentious, but I've been thinking about truffles pretty much non-stop since 2003, so here ya go.

ingredient overview

Some of Our BFF Ingredients

AGAR

Agar (its full name is agar-agar, but we lost the formality long ago) is a real workhorse in our kitchen. It's made from seaweed and is a remarkable vegetarian gelatin substitute. It works by being brought slowly to a boil with a liquid, and is sold in flakes, sticks, and powder. For all uses, the powder is far superior. Agar powder is available in Asian markets (often in small, cheap packets) and in health food stores (often in small, expensive bottles). If you're in a real pickle, you can use the sticks or flakes and grind them as finely as possible in a coffee grinder, but they can clump up more easily than the powder, so be vigilant.

I once worked in a macrobiotic restaurant in Manhattan where I had to make huge vats of kanten—a Japanese macrobiotic fruit pudding made with agar and fruit juice and ideally not much else—daily. Because I was a lowly pastry chef, the line cooks claimed the front burners of the roaring stove for their dashis and noodle-water pots, which I had to lean over while whisking the giant pots. The combination

of gallons of thickening fruit juice and not being able to really see what was happening meant the mixture would periodically leap out of the pot and give me terrific arm burns (all chefs are inordinately impressed by burns, so I didn't mind). When making a small quantity of an agar-thickened dessert like the ones in this book, you shouldn't be at risk of burning, but beware of those bubbling pots.

Aside from the burning thing, agar powder is a real dream to use. I was taught in culinary school that if you don't whisk it practically constantly while it's coming to a boil, the finished product will be grainy with globs of tough agar, but it's actually a forgiving ingredient—we use it almost daily in the shop, and we've never ruined a recipe by underwhisking. Give the pot a vigorous and thorough whisking (making sure to incorporate any stubborn bits on the side of the pot) every few minutes and you should be just fine.

These days we use Genutine instead of plain-Jane agar—Genutine is the brand name for a gelling agent also made from seaweed (carrageenan). It's a little fancier, pricier, more stable, and easier to work with than agar. It creates gels that aren't as brittle as agar. Agar is a hippie gelatin, Genutine is a hipster gelatin. You can substitute either in a 1:1 ratio, depending on what your life choices have led you to at this moment.

CHOCOLATE

This book is about making your own *chocolates*, not your own *chocolate*. That little s changes everything. *Making chocolate* from scratch refers to a laborious and scientific process involving fermented cacao beans, many machines, and lots of time and trial and error. There's an art to making chocolate from scratch, and it's not one that speaks to my strengths—I'm deeply a chocolatier, not a chocolate maker.

You can make all of the sweets in this book from your favorite dark chocolate. Some recipes specify a certain type or brand of chocolate, but usually the differences between types of chocolates used in recipes are a matter of preference. Single-origin chocolates or boutique blends are nice for straight-up tasting, but when you'll be adding other flavors to chocolate, don't worry about buying the superexpensive stuff. Just find a good, ethical chocolate that tastes good to you.

BITTER? SEMI? Some dark chocolate is labeled "bittersweet" and some is labeled "semisweet." Technically, these labels refer to the proportion of sugar used in the chocolate, so semisweet should be sweeter than bittersweet. In reality, these terms have become so muddled as to be pretty much meaningless: your tongue is the best way to tell how sweet or savory a chocolate is. Even when chocolates specify the percentage of cacao present, the number can be wiggly: the remaining percentage isn't just sugar, it's also cocoa butter and (typically) a small amount of an emulsifier, such as soy lecithin, and vanilla, for a rounded flavor and mouthfeel. Depending on the amount of cocoa butter, the kind of cacao beans used, their age, the roasting process they've endured, and a million other factors, two 70% bittersweet bars will taste dramatically different.

Most of the recipes in this book call for just "dark chocolate." Using a 55% or an 80% chocolate will change the flavor of your confection, but as long as you like it, who cares? Most of the bonbons in our shop use a custom blend of chocolate that works out to be around 66%—a good balance of sweet and bitter.

The good news and the bad news in all this is that to find a chocolate you love and want to work with, you might need to taste your way through the entire dark chocolate section of your local fancy food store.

Many chocolate manufacturers sell bulk bags on the Internet that will last a while. Larger supermarkets, specialty food stores, and health food stores can have good prices on bulk chocolate (mine has a nice organic, fair trade Callebaut chocolate in large chunks in the bulk bin section).

STONE-GROUND CHOCOLATE. And don't overlook the stone-ground varieties, though they can be hard to find in bulk. Stone-ground chocolate is the closest to traditional chocolate you can get. It is pleasingly textured (which is a nice way to say "slightly gritty"), with balanced flavors that are often evocative of chocolate's beginnings as a minimally processed ancient Aztec drink: hot chiles, warm cinnamon, even corn. (When customers at the shop exclaim that our Smoky Corn on the Cob Chocolate Bar seems so exotic, we like to explain that, in many ways, it's the most traditional bar we make, considering the flavors that early Mesoamerican chocolates used).

Mexican-style stone-ground chocolate is different from European-style chocolate, where smoothness is all. It's wilder and rougher and more relaxed and I use it whenever I can. Confections come out differently with stone-ground chocolate, since it will never be fully smooth, but that's part of their charm and deliciousness. Stone-ground chocolate tells us to shift our thinking about what chocolate can be used for: it makes good confections that don't pretend to be European-style filled pieces, but have a wabi-sabi punk integrity all their own.

COCONUT

We use full-fat, unsweetened, canned coconut milk and deodorized coconut oil as our primary milk and butter substitutes.

Canned milk! I know. Our coconut is ethically harvested and minimally processed, is a renewable resource, and tastes good. All ingredients are inherently problematic. I'll take the problems that don't involve rape (which is what milk is, hi, those cows don't want to be pregnant all the time, even the ones who are treated so nice) and murder.

We buy our coconut oil a pallet at a time, but a jar might do you fine. Get the deodorized kind. It's a little more processed, but you're going to die anyway someday and it'll ensure that your confections don't taste coconutty. More than butter,

coconut oil is a perfect carrier of flavor—it's a saturated fat, so it takes to infusions spectacularly well, and because its own mild flavor disappears when used as a flavor agent, it carries flavors to your mouth efficiently but politely leaves none of its own, making a Rosemary Sea Salt Caramel shiny with rosemary, salty with salt, not overly, mouth-coatingly buttery.

Nutritionists will tell you a lot about how healthy coconut oil is, but I don't really have a leg to stand on with that, since this is a book about sugar.

SALT

Three types of salt are called for in this book: sea salt, fleur de sel sea salt, and specialty salts. "Sea salt" refers to table salt—any small-grained everyday salt. "Fleur de sel sea salt" is any kind of flaky, large-grained sea salt that you like. Various other specialty salts, such as lemon salt and truffle salt, are specified in individual recipes.

These recipes have a lot of salt by volume because we use a very fluffy, light fleur de sel salt that weighs about half that of regular table salt. If a recipe calls for fleur de sel sea salt but you only have table salt, use the same **weight** if you're measuring in grams, but halve the **measurement**; that is, if a recipe calls for 2 tablespoons/16 grams of fleur de sel sea salt, use 1 tablespoon **or** 16 grams of regular salt.

SUGAR

My hippie childhood and education taught me one great rule: make a treat a treat. So, I do. I don't eat sugar when I'm not eating sugar. No soda or packaged junk with secret sugar. Plus, our confections are so rich and intense and also so tasty that you don't need much of them. That sounds pretentious, but it's true. If you want to pig out on them, though, I won't judge you. I mean, that helps me make payroll and stuff.

This isn't a health food cookbook. Truffles are better for you than caramels, because dark chocolate is better for you than pure sugar and fat. But, still. It's true that the better your treats are, the more intense and wildly satisfying, the less you need to eat. Don't eat a lot of sugar. Eat really, really good sugar. Handmade, vegan, organic, fair trade, interestingly flavored sugar.

There's a weird fact about sugar that all vegans know and almost no nonvegans know: it's not generally vegan. Neither is living in the world at all, so how much you decide to worry about this is somewhat of a sliding scale in the vegan world.

Weirdly, bones are what render sugar nonvegan. Cow bones are charred and used as a whitening agent during the cane sugar refining process. If it's listed on the packaging at all, it's listed as "natural charcoal."

Luckily, avoiding bony sugar is easy: organic cane sugars aren't generally as refined as white sugar and skip the bone process. Many smaller sugar companies don't use it either, nor do noncane sugars, such as like beet sugar or coconut sugar.

As far as types of sugar, we're purists and generally use the classic three: granulated sugar, confectioners' sugar, and brown sugar. Dark maple syrup and rice syrup have found their way into some of our confections, the former more than the latter because it's made locally and also, of course, because it's the most delicious substance on planet Earth (though in moderation because it's also—deservedly so—one of the most expensive).

Our everyday poison of choice is Wholesome Sweeteners Organic Evaporated Cane Juice Sugar. It's great on three fronts: it works just like regular old white sugar, it's organic, and it's fair trade certified.

We also use large quantities of confectioners' (powdered) sugar, generally Florida Crystals brand. Organic confectioners' sugar lacks an additive in conventional sugar that reduces clumping, so it can lump up a bit, especially if exposed to humidity. Processing it for a few seconds in a food processor prior to using or straining de-lumps it nicely.

Light brown and dark brown sugars are nice to work with because some of the work of caramelization is already done for you—they add warm, toasty, autumnal flavors.

VANILLA

We get these amazing organic vanilla beans from this old Jewish hippie guy who lives in Maui (except that he lives in Kauai, this description fits my ex-partner Jacob's father exactly, which endears our vanilla guy to me even more) and hand-pollinates his vanilla orchids in the warm trade winds. He sends us packets of two hundred beans at a time in layers of resealable plastic bags that do nothing to hide their smell from the letter carrier, who always brings envelopes of them inside instead of stuffing them into the mailbox, yelling out, "It's vanilla!" It is vanilla.

However you get your beans, love them and value their power. They aren't cheap and it's such a gift to have them. Store them in the refrigerator, tightly wrapped, to prolong their freshness. When you're about to use them, warm them in the sun, microwave, or low oven for a bit to limber them up before slitting them lengthwise with a sharp paring knife and scraping every trace of beans (technically these are the "beans" and the thing you're scraping them from is the "pod," but, eh. Language is mutable.) from inside the flaps. The leftover, filleted vanilla pod (see?) isn't useless at all—toss it and some friends in a jar filled with vodka to make homemade vanilla extract (steep it for six months, or until it tastes good), or dry it out and grind it up in a spice grinder to make vanilla powder.

Vanilla extract is just vanilla beans aged in alcohol. Use a real one, not artificial vanilla flavor or...well, or else you'll be going to all the trouble of making these fancy confections but using artificial flavor, and what's the purpose of that?

about the recipes

Confectionery recipes are weird. It makes sense to measure some quantities in grams and some in teaspoons. At our shop, we have two scales, one that measures in either grams, pounds, or ounces, and one that measures in one-tenth-of-a-gram increments. Instead of asking you to buy two scales, just measure larger quantities in grams and smaller ones in teaspoons and tablespoons. Each recipe also has measurements for cups, in case you don't have a scale, but read here about why you should get a cheap scale.

Professional American confectionery recipes typically measure liquids by volume in millimeters, but we use grams just because that's what we do in our shop and we've never had a problem (we list cup and tablespoon measurements, too).

AN IMPORTANT NOTE ABOUT POT SIZES

These recipes call for pots of various sizes. **Cooking a confectionery recipe in a too-small or too-big pot can make a huge difference in your finished product.** Pots that are too small can make your recipe bubble over easily (so. much. sticky. cleaning.), and pots that are too wide can cause a recipe to evaporate before it caramelizes. Caramel and toffee in particular are unlike making soup or pasta sauce in that they need a lot of space to "grow" as they cook, so a pot that looks overly tall for a recipe might be just right.

If you're unsure how many quarts your pots hold, fill them up with water using a 4-cup liquid measure (1 quart) or, if it's all you have, a cup measure (4 cups is 1 quart) or a gallon jug (4 quarts is 1 gallon). Make a list and tape it up to your kitchen cabinets for future use, if you want. In our shop we used to use a Seinfeld system of pot naming, whereby all our recipes instructed one to cook a recipe in either Jerry, Kramer, George, or Elaine, then we began to feel this was a little body shaming (and also started employing humans born long after Seinfeld was a thing) and moved to a colored electrical tape system whereby 8-quart pots have a yellow tape ring around their handles; 12-quart, blue tape, and so on.

If you like to cook, invest in good pots. I still have my battered All-Clad pots from culinary school twenty years ago, and I use them every day at work and home. I've thrown them during rages in my pretherapy days (not **at** anyone, just alone at midnight when entering a fifteenth-hour-of-work sort of night), I've burnt countless pots of caramel in them; they've seen it all, from endless caramelized onion piles to exhaustion tears to truffle béchamels to the daintiest ganaches. Cheap pots can also have hot spots that cause a caramel to cook unevenly. They'll work in a pinch, but if you make a lot of caramel, (1) orange you glad I wrote you this book, and (2) buy some good pots, okay?

NECESSARY AND HELPFUL TOOLS

I was about twenty-three when I first baked a cake in layers in two parchment paper–lined springform cake pans (instead of the dented and slightly rusty old-fashioned one-piece pan I bought at a yard sale while in college and made layer cakes by eyeballing half the cake and cutting it in half horizontally—after working hard to free the stuck cake from the sides of the pan) and frosted using an offset spatula (instead of a butter knife) while luxuriously spinning on a cake stand (instead of inverting it onto a concave dinner plate and rotating it after frosting every half inch). It felt like finally exhaling after holding my breath for ages. I slowly discovered that making sweets can be pleasurable not just for the recipient but for the maker.

Unlike baking, chocolate making doesn't require many special tools: no cake pans, cake stands, fiddly pastry tips to get lost in the dishwasher—rarely do chocolate makers even use an oven. Many of our most-used tools come from a hardware store. Most of the recipes in this book can be made using everyday kitchen equipment (bowls, spoons, spatulas, a pot now and then), but a few cheap tools from a local restaurant supply or (if you want to spend more) a kitchenware shop will improve your chocolate making experience intensely. A few tools can be the difference between confections that are a pleasure to produce and ones that are a pain.

If you splurge on one tool to make the confections in this book, make it a kitchen scale. Most of all, a **digital kitchen scale** will make chocolate making much quicker and easier: no dirtying of endless measuring cups and spoons, just breezily putting ingredients onto a waiting scale. A great digital kitchen scale costs around $25—we use Escali scales, which come in lovely colors, too. Be sure that your scale measures grams as well as ounces and pounds. Recipes in this book are listed in cups as well as grams. You will be so much happier in your kitchen with a scale, particularly when using this book.

Bench scrapers are unexpectedly useful for candy making. We use a dedicated one for scraping up the floor at the end of the night (actually, it's a paint scraper)—nothing else gets up bits of hard chocolate or caramel as easily—but we also use untold numbers of them for ensuring molds full of chocolates have an even top coating of chocolate and that molds full of caramels are absolutely filled to the top without wasteful caramel pooled on the sides, as well as cleaning counters efficiently. When you have a few bench scrapers around, you'll find more and more uses for them. Need a bench scraper? Available for a dollar or so at kitchen supply shops.

A **coffee grinder** is, strangely, one of our most frequently used kitchen tools. In this book I call it a spice grinder, and it's used not just for spices but for dried vegetables and herbs that we use often. Just get a simple $20 blade grinder, not a fancy burr grinder. You can clean it easily by whizzing some dried rice in it afterward and wiping out with a paper towel. If you are obsessed with reducing food waste, you can then make the world's smallest rice congee with your spiced rice by cooking it in hot water like pasta, but mostly we just throw it out, with me yelling at everyone to take it home in a little bag and cook it up.

Truffle **dipping wands** and **forks** are nice to have, but not essential unless you're dipping more than a few dozen candies. The tiny basket-shaped wands cradle round truffles as they journey into tempered chocolate for their chocolate coating, and the flat forks are excellent for hand-dipping caramels and other flat or square confections.

If you're planning on making a lot of the caramel recipes in this book, buy a few **silicone molds** for caramel instead of having to fiddle with cutting the caramel into squares, which will for sure drive you bananas. The very best molds are firm silicone designed for caramel. We get ours from JB Prince in a 7/8-inch square cavity size, but there are many places to buy them online (search for "professional candy mold" or "professional caramel mold"). Be sure they're dishwasher-safe and heat-safe up to 350°F.

A roll (or sheets) of **parchment paper** is essential for keeping trays clean and giving chocolate a stick-free surface to set up on. Waxed paper will work also, but parchment is somehow tidier, and recycled unbleached parchment is available now, which is nice.

Confectionery work requires a strangely large number of **sheet pans**. The more you have, the happier you will be. Quarter-size sheet pans (13 by 9 inches) and half sheet pans (18 by 13 inches) work well for home confectioners, but a few full-size sheet pans (26 by 18 inches), if you have the space to store them, will provide a luxuriously large expanse for truffle dipping or ganache rolling. Sheet pans are cheap; buy a lot. In a pinch, dented cookie sheets and trays of all kinds can work, but sheet pans are great because of their small lip, which keep truffles from rolling away.

Offset spatulas are useful in the chocolate kitchen. These are small spatulas (we prefer the petite sizes) cantilevered to spread chocolate, frosting, or caramel neatly.

A good candy **thermometer** is an essential for making caramel and candies of all kinds—except ganache-based chocolates, such as truffles. A supermarket candy thermometer will set you back around $4 and will work okay, but a digital instant-read thermometer is much more pleasurable to use, though costing a bit more. Be sure to always wash thermometers (or soak the probe in hot water) immediately after use, to prevent molten hot sugar from sticking to them.

temper, temper: starring theobroma cacao as herself

Tempered Chocolate Is Beautiful,

and It Can Also Drive You Bananas

— —

At our shop, the first thing we teach people is how to tell between properly tempered and out-of-temper chocolate. Tempered chocolate is glossy, snappy, and smooth. Not all tempered chocolate looks the same, however: Aztec-style craft bean-to-bar chocolate is often not conched, or ground, as long as European ultra-smooth, ultraconched chocolate, and it tends to have a more matte look (and different flavor, in a good way, from European-style chocolate).

Hand-dipped truffles and caramels will always be more matte than chocolates made in molds. Molded chocolates are shinier because the chocolate is in contact with the cradling surface of the mold, which holds the temper better, until completely dry.

Out-of-temper chocolate looks a lot of different ways: it can be slightly marbled with white streaks, a little dull, or dusty and powdery looking. If you've ever left a chocolate bar in a hot car and then put it in a refrigerator to firm it up again, you've seen chocolate that's out of temper.

There's a long technical explanation I could go into to explain what happens when chocolate gets out of temper, but in short: out-of-temper chocolate is angry chocolate whose molecules have gotten all out of whack: literally, it's lost its temper.

Here's the thing, though: your chocolate might get mad if you don't treat it the way it wants to be treated, but it will still taste great.

Tempering chocolate is necessary for a perfect shiny finish for your truffles and other confections, but if you're making treats just for kicks, it'll still taste just fine if you skip the tempering step.

It's important to start with chocolate that has a nice temper—don't remelt any old, bloomy chocolate bar until you're a tempering pro—start with fresh, shiny dark chocolate. You can chop up a good-quality chocolate bar, or use *callets* (pieces), which are often available in the bulk section of supermarkets or fancy food shops. In our shop our base chocolate is a 66%, which has a nice all-purpose flavor.

Here we go. Tempering is one of those things in life, like, you know, having a child or whatever, that you hold in your heart forever and are proud of when the world is trying to tear you down: you know that you can temper chocolate, so how much can any other junk really affect you?

It's not that scary, really.

Okay, let's start aligning some molecules.

Get some dark chocolate, a pound. You can temper half as much, you can temper twice as much. If you're making one recipe of truffles, you only need about 8 ounces (half a pound) or less of tempered chocolate to dip them. I like to temper a lot because then you have a good quantity of seed chocolate (well-tempered chocolate you can use to "teach" untempered chocolate how to behave properly) *and*, once you have nicely tempered chocolate on hand, you can use it for most applications by barely melting it and using it without retempering, as long as it doesn't zoom above its temper temperature (around 87°F).

The following temperatures are average temperatures for tempering dark chocolate. If you're in possession of fancy nouveau chocolate that lists the best temperatures for tempering on the package, go by those temperatures instead.

Put two thirds of the chocolate (roughly 11 ounces) in a metal bowl (glass works, too) over some barely, barely simmering water or a double boiler. Stir with a spatula slowly and gently while monitoring the temperature. Don't let it get above 120°F. Don't let it zoom up right to 120°F over furiously boiling water, because it'll keep getting warmer as it heats up. Turn off the heat at around 116°F and let it float up to 120°F. If it doesn't, keep the water gently simmering.

Take the chocolate off the heat. Be extra careful and towel off the bottom of the bowl. Water is the enemy of chocolate, always (see: Laura Esquivel). Gently stir in the remaining one third of the chocolate (roughly 5 ounces), called seed chocolate, a little at a time, letting each new addition melt before adding more. Seed chocolate is well-tempered chocolate that teaches the melted chocolate how to behave. The idea is that its nicely snappy molecules melt just enough to mingle well but not enough to fall out of temper, and the out-of-temper molecules it's added to will fall into line because of its good example. Seed chocolate is your ally, your tempering BFF.

Don't wildly whisk your seed chocolate in, don't energetically beat it in, just shimmer it in with the spatula—be the benevolent overlord facilitating these two parts becoming one. This all sounds sort of superstitious. Welcome to the world of chocolate work.

Let the chocolate cool to 80° to 82°F. If your chocolate cools before you've added in all the seed chocolate, that's okay. Don't freak out if it's cooler, just begin warming it over the double boiler. If it seems as if it's never going to get to 82°F, keep gently stirring with your spatula to incorporate air and cool it down. When it's at 82°F, start warming it again, real gently this time (how many times can I mention to be gentle?), until it comes to 88°F, or if you want to be really precise, 88.7°F. For some reason, some people at this stage put a little chocolate under their bottom lip, supposedly the most sensitive part of the body. The chocolate should feel cool on your chin, since it's about 10°F below body temperature. Invariably you're going to forget that chocolate is there.

YOU'RE DONE! Now use it ASAP, before it falls out of temper. A good working temperature range for tempered chocolate is 86°–90°F. If it gets too cool to work with, gently warm it, attempting to stay within the temper range. If your chocolate gets too cool and starts firming up, you'll need to re-temper, with fresh seed chocolate that has a good temper (I superstitiously only use factory-tempered fresh chocolate that's never been melted as seed chocolate, but if you have leftover chocolate that has a good snap and shine, use it as your seed). You can re-temper forever.

To test your temper, smear a little chocolate on a spoon or piece of parchment paper and let it set up in the fridge for a few minutes, until it's set (or crystallized, as we say "in the industry"). Inspect it for white streaks. If it's shiny and snappy, you're ready to go.

● · ● · ● · ●

ganache is a sonnet

Ganache is a sonnet, or maybe a haiku. How pretentious! But still. A small thing. A few lines, three ingredients, that evoke the universe. Endlessly versatile whether licked off a spoon or poured onto a cake to make a mirror-shiny frosting lake. Queen of the chocolate universe.

The story is that truffles were invented when French housewives had little bits of ganache to use up. They rolled them in cocoa powder and voilà. Who has leftover bits of ganache to use up (other than chocolate shops)? French housewives?

When we're training new chocolatiers-to-be at our shop, here's how we explain ganache: ganache is simple, but simple is not the same as easy (this mantra works for a lot of chocolate and sugarwork; it works also for everything in your life). Ganache takes five minutes to make, but even after making it regularly for fifteen years, I'm still learning from it. I like that.

The good news is that, like a lot in the chocolate world, even imperfect ganache is still ridiculously tasty. It's also one of the most fun and quick desserts you can make. It's the basis for almost half of the recipes in this book, so let's spend some time on it.

Ganache is traditionally made with chocolate, cream, and sometimes butter. If you expand the definitions of "butter" and "cream" to mean "a fat" and "a liquid," you can make ganache a million ways and most of them will be amazing.

Chocolate + grapeseed oil + carrot juice? Chocolate + beet puree + almond milk? Chocolate + olive oil + beer? A French housewife might have a bone to pick with you, but in the modern pastry world all of these are ganaches, and I've made them all, and they've all been great. I've added flavorings to ganache that range from smoked eggplant to homemade miso to balsamic syrup (with a hundred kinds of bougie salt in between), and usually they work—it's just a matter of tweaking to get the flavors to work well together.

Back to ganache. Most of our ganache recipes use coconut oil and coconut milk as the fat and liquid. Our master ganache recipe uses slightly less coconut oil, proportionally, than traditional recipes, because coconut oil is decadently 100 percent saturated fat, with none of the milk solids that cause trouble when working with butter.

This ganache recipe scales up gorgeously. You can multiply it by two or ten and have ganache to last a while. However, ganache is so easy to make, and so much easier to work with when freshly made (before it hardens into a fudgy solid) that it makes more sense to make it as needed. Ganache, like anything made of chocolate, is also a sensitive soul that loves to try on any other flavors nearby in the refrigerator or freezer—so if you do refrigerate or freeze it, wrap it well and keep it away from those caramelized onions you're saving for tomorrow night's soup (unless you're making Chipotle and Caramelized Onion Truffles, page 57).

The technique for ganache is simple: heat your liquid and fat together (let this mixture boil a little, to kill any harmful organisms that might be lurking around and to make your ganache last longer). Turn off the heat. Add your chocolate, chopped into small pieces. Slowly whisk until the chocolate is incorporated and you've made a smooth emulsion.

Smoothness is the thing here. A lumpy ganache isn't really ganache. Ganache should melt slowly and evenly on the tongue, uninterrupted by chunky chocolate. If you're unsure, taste a little, mashing it between your tongue and hard palate to check for a smooth texture.

On the other hand, beating the ganache wildly can cause it to seize up or break: it will harden quickly and unevenly into a lumpen mass, or separate into an oily mess. Seized ganache is fixable by reheating it gently over a double boiler or in a microwave set to low power, then rewhisking, more gently this time, until smooth and creamy again. If possible, while whisking, add a few teaspoons of warmed coconut milk, a little at a time, or perfect, fluid melted ganache, but if you have perfect ganache just hanging out, you should probably go make something with that before it firms up and worry about the seized ganache later.

Ganache rewards attention: it's easy to work with when soft and stirrable, but once it sets up and is firm, it needs to be gently remelted (using the same technique for seized ganache) to be flavored or piped into truffle centers.

At our shop, we have a rule: **do what ganache wants when it wants it**. Don't fight with ganache; there's no reason. When it's ready to be piped, just pipe it. Be the river rocks yielding to what the river wants, floating with the current. If someone is making truffles and also helping customers, they let someone else know to pipe their truffles when a squeeze of the pastry bag tells them they're ready to be piped. (So many tasks at the chocolate shop remind me of double Dutch: I've been jumping for a while but I've got to get out, so watch for the rhythm and jump in when you can, okay?)

A note on water: the primary rule of chocolate work is not to allow the chocolate to come into contact with water, but this doesn't apply to ganache, which is tempered with liquid already. A few drops of water in the form of a wet spoon or bowl won't hurt a bit.

You can flavor ganache in two ways: **infusions**, and **additions**. **Infusions** are added to the milk and oil as the ganache is being made; **additions** are added to a finished ganache. Different ingredients lend themselves to each technique. Tender herbs will be lost if you just chop them up and add them to finished ganache. But if they're quickly infused into the milk, their flavor will shine through. Alcohols, which make ganache softer, smoother, last longer, and taste better, should always be added after the cooking is finished so their heat-sensitive flavors don't evaporate.

Truffles, ganache bonbons, and drinking chocolates are the primary use for fresh ganache in our shop, but ganache also makes frostings (smooth and whipped), mousses, fillings, sauces, and more—you'll see. Ganache keeps for two months in the freezer or one week in the refrigerator.

The master recipe makes enough to make roughly two of the truffle flavors that follow. If you're making ganache, you might as well make some more ganache, right? So, either halve this recipe or stash the extra in the freezer, where it will keep for several months.

Let's go.

ganache master recipe

Makes 45 to 50 truffles (enough for 2 of the recipes that follow)

¾ cup plus 2 tablespoons/200 g full-fat coconut milk

¼ cup/45 g refined coconut oil

1 tablespoon/10 g water

2 cups/345 g dark chocolate, chopped into small pieces

1. Place the milk, oil, and water in a 2- to 4-quart pot and bring to a full boil over medium heat. Turn off the heat when the mixture just begins to climb the pot.
2. Add the chocolate; gently swirl the pan to cover the chocolate with the milk, but do not stir. Cover the pot. Let stand, undisturbed, for 1 to 2 minutes.
3. Slowly whisk until the mixture is combined and uniform.

TRUFFLES

I sort of love how *truffle* has become shorthand for "a round thing." Or "a fancy candy thing." We've come to realize that people coming to our shop asking for truffles aren't necessarily asking for nubbly ganache-based confections; they just want a nice piece of candy. Or they do want a truffle, and are annoyed when we try to sell them a Tahini Meltaway. The art of customer service involves a lot of mind reading. Don't get me started on macaroon vs. macaron.

In the Lagusta's Luscious–verse, the only thing we sell under the truffle name is ganache piped into little piles of goo that are rolled between our hands and dipped in small bowls of tempered chocolate. We've been reduced to only making truffles as special treats because of their week-long shelf life and laughably, profit-killingly high labor costs.

The reasons that make truffles a somewhat ridiculous offering in a chocolate shop (even one as ludicrously, anarchistically unconcerned with profit-making as ours) are the reasons they're easy and fun to make at home: no special equipment needed, just your hands and a little time. Truffles are the best, man.

The best part of truffle making is truffle garnishing. Truffle garnishing—argh, I don't even know how to start this. Is it getting warm in here? Why is my heart palpitating all of the sudden? I love garnishing truffles. I was never cool in high school, can you tell? I love adding tiny twee precious little bits and pieces to tiny things lined up in precise rows. Truffle making can be messy, but garnishing is so clean. A bowl of a small garnishes,

a truffle dipper, a bowl of tempered chocolate, and a sheet pan of truffles. The world feels orderly, creative on a manageable scale. Look at all these darling little balls lined up on this sheet pan! I feel accomplished and calm.

There are three primary methods for truffle garnishing. You can dip your truffles into chocolate and sprinkle them with your garnish (or precisely place it on the top of the truffle, with your fingers or chopsticks or tweezers), or you can roll your truffle into a garnish meant to completely encase it (cocoa powder is the most classic of these), or you can set it into a bed of a garnishing substance. Setting truffles into a bed or rolling them around in a tasty substance can be a way to add another layer of flavor to your truffle. Garnishing them with a sprinkle adds striking visual interest.

Your garnish can nod to the flavor of your truffle, or it can add another element of flavor. Or you can incorporate a swirl of chocolate or other old-fashioned design when lifting the truffle off the dipping fork that becomes your garnish, or you can make an interesting texture by rolling your dipped truffle on something called an impression mat (a nubbly silicone mat with a special design printed on it—I bet if you look around your house or kitchen, you'll find something similar—a particularly textured clean towel, or basket?) or colander or fine-screened strainer or cooling rack.

When pressing a substantial garnish onto a truffle, we add a little "seatbelt" for stability, made of chocolate: our ginger truffles are garnished with a tiny piece of crystallized ginger, so when we press the ginger into the truffle, we use a finger

Beet-Coriander Truffles (page 56)

to quickly grab a bit of the liquid chocolate and fold it over the garnish, securing it in place, or at least looking kind of cool.

Spend a little time thinking about your truffle garnishes. It's a nice opportunity to use something really special. You only need the tiniest quantity of garnishing material, so you can splurge a little. Instead of just sprinkling on some dried coconut, maybe get a fresh mature coconut, shave off some slices with a vegetable peeler, and use big pieces as a garnish, placing them artfully askew like cool art deco hats.

Some things you could sprinkle on your truffles:

- Coarsely ground cinnamon (I like canela, a.k.a. "Mexican cinnamon." It's soft and can be broken into tiny mini sticks that look cool.)
- Any other nice spice on the planet, coarsely ground
- Chopped chocolate (how meta)
- Sprinkles!
- Fancy sea salt: smoked, lemon-infused, tea-infused, interestingly sized, shaped, and tasting sea salts of all kinds make unbelievable truffle garnishes. Check out your local specialty food store for a nice selection, or themeadow.com.
- Harissa or other spice mixes, homemade or not; just make sure they're fresh.
- Tea—herbal, green, black, blends, oolong, pu'er, anything beautiful and tasty
- Chile powders (not chili powder, the mix of chiles and spices meant for chili, but powders made from one kind of chile), such as ancho, chipotle, pasilla, or maybe a very little cayenne. Don't let me dissuade you from using chili powder if you feel like it too, though.

- Coffee beans, whole or smashed into smaller pieces
- Citrus zest
- Candied citrus zest (when garnishing with anything candied, be sure to consume soon before things get sticky)
- Candied citrus slices or pieces
- Lavender (don't go crazy)
- Edible flower petals
- Mint leaves, candied mint leaves, or chocolate mint leaves (brush tempered chocolate onto mint leaves, peel away the leaf when the chocolate is set)
- Toasted coconut (shreds or flakes are both nice)
- Chopped, toasted nuts or seeds
- A squiggle or swirl or swoosh of tempered chocolate
- Crystallized rose petals or violets, which you can buy online or in specialty confectionery shops
- Seaweed, particularly dulse or smoked dulse or nori
- Foraged things: fennel pollen, cattail pollen, spicebush powder, dried bee balm flowers, dried dame's rocket flowers, dried wild violets, dried wild bergamot flowers, other foraged or purchased pollens or wild herb or spice powders
- Fancy sugars, such as turbinado or other large-crystal sugars. Use these only if your truffles are going to be eaten soon, before the sugar gets sticky.

Some things you could use to make a bed to drop truffles into or to roll truffles in:

- Toasted coconut (shreds or flakes are both nice)

- Chopped, toasted nuts or seeds
- Confectioners' sugar
- Dehydrated apple skin, coarsely ground in a spice grinder
- Many other dehydrated or freeze-dried fruit and vegetable peels, coarsely ground
- Fruit and vegetable powders (made from dehydrated or freeze-dried fruits and vegetables), finely ground
- Chopped or shaved or powdered chocolate
- Coffee or espresso
- Tea (matcha or other finely-ground teas)

Learn from my mistakes and do not use the following as truffle garnishes:

- Crushed candy canes (stickiness)
- Crushed candy of any kind (stickiness)
- Saffron threads (they won't taste like anything and you're wasting a lot of money)
- Whole star anise (no)
- Big whole peppercorns (hard no)
- Any other giant whole inedible spice

truffles master recipe

Makes 20 to 25 truffles

1 cup/260 g ganache (page 25)
½ pound chocolate, for dipping
Desired flavor topping (pages 35–67)
Garnishes

1. Flavor your ganache as directed in the individual flavor recipes, then let the ganache sit at room temperature, stirring often, until firm enough to pipe, 30 minutes or so after being made: it should hold its shape when lifted with a spoon instead of pouring off, and feel semisolid, changing from an initial thick hand lotion consistency to a sort of thicker toothpaste kind of thing. If you're working in a hot space (above 65°F), you can refrigerate the ganache, but it sets up fast in the refrigerator—watch it!

2. Line a sheet pan with parchment or waxed paper. Use a pastry bag fitted with a ½-inch tip or a disposable pastry bag (or resealable plastic bag) cut to make a ½-inch opening to pipe centers. Use a plastic bench scraper to scrape the ganache down to the bottom of the bag periodically, so you're not wasting your precious ganache. Or forget the pastry bag nonsense and let the ganache firm up a little more and spoon out your truffle centers. It's a little more time-consuming, but just fine.

3. Pipe the ganache into walnut-size truffle centers. Really the only thing that matters when piping is that you get those babies out of the pastry bag in some semblance of solidity. You can resize them later. Just go for good solid masses without hollow centers and don't stress too much about size consistency right now. Pipe a straight, sure-footed plop of ganache (yes, I know exactly what it looks like), not tiered hollow-centered beehives. If you're making multiple flavors, be sure to label the parchment paper sheet with the flavor names, lest you have to pinch off tiny bits of each one and taste them to remember what you were doing. If your ganache slides right out of the pastry bag, knead it a little and let it sit a few more minutes. If it's too firm to pipe, pipe it anyway, because your hands on the pastry bag will warm it up.

4. Let the truffle centers set up at room temperature until firm. This is a good time to assemble all your garnishes and tools for dipping.

5. Roll the centers between your palms (rinse your hands often in cold water, then dry them thoroughly) to make round truffle centers. If necessary, resize the centers by pulling off pieces

from larger balls and rolling them onto smaller ones to ensure uniformity. You're looking at 11 to 13 grams apiece, but who's counting. Line up your centers like good little soldiers on a parchment-lined sheet pan.

6. At this point, you can let your ganaches sit at room temperature for a few hours or a day or so.

7. Temper the chocolate (see page 17). To dip each truffle recipe (25 truffles or so), you'll need 4 to 8 ounces of fluid tempered chocolate.

8. This step is optional, but it's nice to give softer ganaches an extra chocolate layer to guard against weeping, seeping, or cracking their final chocolate shell: with your hands, roll each truffle center in a tiny bit of tempered chocolate (barely melted out-of-temper chocolate will be fine also; for heaven's sake, don't temper chocolate just for this step). Let cool on a parchment-covered sheet pan.

9. At this point, have all your tools and garnishes nearby and be prepared to work quickly, because chocolate hardens fast.

10. Dip one cooled truffle center into the melted tempered chocolate, using a truffle dipper, a fork, or your fingers (I prefer a truffle dipper, which will only set you back a few dollars, and my fingers. A fork will drive you up a wall). Let any excess chocolate drop back into the tempered chocolate bowl. Or roll the center in another coat of tempered chocolate with your hands, for a more rustic effect.

11. Your truffle dipper or hands or fork will quickly become unusable with hardened chocolate, so either have many on hand, or wash and dry them completely in between batches. Working quickly helps with this, too. To efficiently release your truffle from the dipper, give it a good definitive tap on the side of the sheet pan.

12. Place the truffle in the desired flavor topping. With a spoon, cover the truffle with the topping. Let sit in the bowl for a few minutes. Alternatively, dip the truffles onto a parchment sheet and spoon the topping over them. Garnish as desired.

13. Truffles should be eaten within 1 week, otherwise the perishable ganache center could get moldy. For longer storage, store piped, unrolled truffle centers in the freezer. Bring to room temperature and towel off to ensure they're dry before dipping. Roll and dip as many as will be consumed within a week.

Dark Chocolate and Fruity Truffles

Dark chocolate ganache + fruit. Best + best.

Fruit makes ganache softer, so the trick with making fruity truffles is adding enough fruit to flavor the ganache but not enough to make the ganache too liquid to pipe, roll, and dip in chocolate. Since all fruits vary in sweetness and moisture levels, you might need to modify your ganaches as necessary to make your fruity truffles firm up properly—add fruit flavoring to taste, don't worry about following the recipe too closely. With some exceptions, I like to use fresh (or fresh-frozen) fruit in ganaches; fresh fruit gives you a superbright, fruit-forward flavor that's true to the flavor of the fruit.

Freezing fruit is a great way to economically preserve your farmers' market haul for more lean times of year, but often fruit frozen in a home freezer becomes a lumpen watery mass over time. To prevent this, use the Individual Quick Freeze technique: Line a sheet pan small enough to fit in your freezer with parchment paper, then spread the fruit on it in one layer without any pieces touching. Freeze for two to three hours—until the fruit is frozen, but not so long that it becomes freezer-burnt and develops ice crystals. Pack the frozen fruit into thick resealable plastic bags and squeeze out all remaining air. Or vacuum-seal the bags—small but effective vacuum sealers are available in kitchenware shops and will keep fruit fresher than any other method.

Another technique for making extremely fruity ganache without losing its essential texture is to add some fresh fruit and some freeze-dried, powdered fruit. Freeze-dried fruit powders are in every health food store and you can even get organic ones. If you can't find the powder, just grind up the regular freeze-dried fruits in a spice or coffee grinder. Mix some of the powder into ganache in combination with fresh fruit puree to add another layer of fruit flavor. Your fruit powder can also become a truffle garnish, which adds another bit of flavor, color, and good textural contrast to the truffle.

Sometimes fruity truffles leak a little after being dipped in chocolate. You're free to not care about this at all. If you've really pushed the fruit flavor of your ganache, they can even crack, oozing ganache out of the opening. This can affect their perishability, but since truffles should be eaten fairly quickly anyway, this is mostly a cosmetic problem. Truffles aren't meant to be perfect, anyway; think of their knobbly namesake: only roughly round, oozing earth. What matters is the flavor.

black (or red) raspberry–lime truffles

· ·

One year, a farmer kept bringing us beautiful black raspberries he had grown. They were full of hard, unforgiving seeds, but otherwise the flavor was spectacular. I bought all he had. We froze a lot for unspecified future projects, figuring we would puree and strain them just before use. One of our chocolatiers, Dawnmarie, was making Raspberries de Pizan, a raspberry bonbon that uses whole red raspberries, and accidentally grabbed a bag of the black raspberries instead. These Raspberries de Pizan were many moons too seedy to use, and their flavor wasn't right, not Raspberry de Pizan enough, something else entirely.

We never throw out mistakes. Our ingredients are too expensive, and it's a good opportunity to stretch yourself and see what you can make of a screw-up. Maresa took what she had made and reverse engineered it into a workable truffle. People went sort of wild for it—an easy, flavor-bomb truffle, tart with lime and raspberry, and the strawberry powder layer zinged it up nicely.

This ganache is the only one we ever add sugar to. It works, though. To really push the fruit flavor to its maximum, we pull out two tricks: cocoa butter and agar powder, both added to stabilize and firm the ganache. Cocoa butter is what makes chocolate set up so nicely at room temperature, so adding plain cocoa butter to a recipe is a chocolate maker's trick to goose a good texture. It has a waxy flavor, though, so don't go overboard. Most health food stores sell organic, fair trade cocoa butter. It keeps forever.

Makes 20 truffles

1½ teaspoons/10 g balsamic syrup (recipe follows)

½ cup/75 g black (or red) raspberries, fresh or frozen

½ teaspoon/3 g agar or Genutine powder

3 tablespoons/40 g coconut milk

2 tablespoons/16 g cocoa butter

½ cup plus 2 tablespoons/100 g chopped bittersweet chocolate

½ teaspoon/1 g culinary-grade lime oil (not extract or essential oil)

½ cup plus 2 tablespoons/75 g confectioners' sugar

Garnish: ½ cup/75 g strawberry powder

1. Combine the syrup, raspberries, agar, milk, and cocoa butter in a 2- to 4-quart pot. Slowly bring to a boil, stirring often, then remove from the heat. Add the chocolate and lime oil and cover the container. Let sit for 5 minutes, then whisk until the chocolate is incorporated.
2. If your raspberries are very seedy, quickly (while it's still warm) push the ganache through a fine-mesh strainer to remove the seeds. (If you get nice black raspberries, you'll want to strain the ganache. If you have soft, gentle, cultivated red raspberries, skip this step.)
3. Puree the confectioners' sugar in a food processor (or sift) to break up any lumps, then add the raspberry ganache to the food processor (or combine in a bowl with the sifted sugar).
4. Taste and adjust the flavors as necessary.
5. Form into truffles as directed in the Truffles Master Recipe (page 31), piping the mixture quickly before it firms up and rolling each dipped truffle in the strawberry powder as it is dipped, or sprinkling a little on top.

• — ⚬ — • — ⚬ — •

Balsamic Syrup

Balsamic syrup keeps indefinitely in the freezer and is nice to have around for drizzling on everything in your life. This recipe makes more than you need, but you can also use it on toast, strawberries, creamy desserts, pie, stone fruit, biscuits, a salad, roasted vegetables, broiled tofu, children wandering into the kitchen—all of it. Every time we make a huge vat of balsamic syrup at the shop, it sets off our smoke alarm (the scaled-down recipe here won't cause any alarms, though it's a good idea to open the windows before making it, because of the pungency). It's exciting stuff.

½ cup/133 g balsamic vinegar

¼ cup/50 g sugar

1. Bring the vinegar and sugar to a boil in a 2-quart pot, then lower the heat to a bare simmer. Cook gently, testing the syrup often by pouring into a measuring cup. The syrup will continue to reduce slightly even after being taken off the heat, so take it off when it's about ⅓ cup, and it will continue reducing on its own. In the end, you want it to be reduced to ¼ cup.
2. Let cool and store in a small container; store in the fridge if you're using within 2 weeks or freeze forever.

blueberry-black currant truffles

The Hudson Valley, and particularly New Paltz, where our shop is, is a blueberry world. College kids and old hippies and homeschooling families and Brooklynites with foraging-focused Instagram accounts[1] hike up to wild blueberry patches along the Shawangunk Ridge and emerge with packs swollen with tiny feral contraband berries. You're technically not allowed to harvest the blueberries, but enforcement is lax and a small band of hardscrabble back-to-the-land nouveau anarcho-punks make a living doing just that.

I (a fake back-to-the-land anarcho-punk who holds a mortgage and employs many people and is a huge hypocrite) usually spend a few afternoons in July picking blueberries up on the mountains, to be made into a jammy puree to use in these truffles. Don't tell.

These truffles burst with blueberry flavor and are pretty much just as terrific made with cultivated blueberries as foraged wild ones. Like the Black (or Red) Raspberry-Lime Truffles (page 35), they can be a bit soft, but the flavor is worth the annoyance.

Cassis is a black currant liqueur available in wine shops. Blueberry powder can be made by grinding freeze-dried blueberries (available in most health food stores) in a spice (coffee) grinder until powdery. If your blueberries are too moist to grind, let them dry out by setting them in your oven turned to the lowest temperature for half an hour or so until crispier, but watch closely so they don't burn.

Makes 20 to 25 truffles

1 cup/260 g ganache (page 25)

2 teaspoons/8 g cassis

3 tablespoons/65 g blueberry jam, store-bought or from recipe that follows

Garnish: blueberry powder

---

1. *An exact, accurate cross-section of New Paltz, New York.*

1. Place all the ingredients, except the garnish, in a medium-size bowl and stir together until emulsified.
2. Taste and adjust the flavor as necessary—though be aware that the more cassis and jam are added, the softer the ganache will be.
3. Form into truffles as directed in the Truffles Master Recipe (page 31).
4. To garnish, sprinkle with a little blueberry powder, or drop each truffle into a shallow container of blueberry powder, then turn upside down once set, for a blueberry top.

Blueberry Jam

This really isn't blueberry jam, but blueberries are so filled with pectin that just heating them with some sugar and letting them hang out for a while makes a workable fake.

Makes ⅓ cup/100 g jam

2 cups/320 g blueberries, fresh or frozen
½ cup/100 g sugar

1. Combine the blueberries and sugar in a 2-quart pot and bring to a boil, then let simmer for 10 minutes, or until the blueberries thicken and break down a little.
2. Remove from the heat. Let cool, then strain (save the juices to stir into vegan yogurt, pour over vegan ice cream, or mix with seltzer for a blueberry soda). Store in the refrigerator 1 week or for 2 months in the freezer.

fennel-apple skin truffles

The Hudson Valley is known for its apples, so we make a lot of apple-focused confections: an apple caramel that uses pureed Pink Lady apples, a spicy apple caramel, an Autumnal Pagan Bark with dried local apple wheels, and these truffles, which use a locally made apple liqueur as well as the skins from the apples used for the apple caramels.

I'm a real apple skin evangelist. It's pretty and it tastes great, as long as you've used a tasty apple variety (no Red Delicious, um). Tart apples are always good for confectionery purposes; they cut through sugar so well. We peel our apples and dehydrate the skin or just let it hang out on a sheet pan for a few days until it's crispy and completely dried out. Then, we grind it coarsely in a spice grinder. You want to stop short of it becoming a powder—some textured, bigger pieces add nice flavor and interest.

We garnish these truffles with fennel pollen and set them, apple skin side down, in a candy cup, so the extra flavor and color of the apple skin become a surprise when the eater picks up the truffle.

Fennel pollen is expensive, but it makes a nice garnish for all kinds of dishes—it has a light, pure fennel flavor that even people who "hate fennel" can tolerate. If you grow fennel, you have a free source of fennel pollen. Just monitor your fennel when it begins to bloom, and when you see lots of pollen on the blossoms, put a sheet on the ground underneath them and shake off all the pollen. Leave it out at room temperature to dry it out, and it's ready to use.

If you don't want to mess with fennel pollen, you can garnish the truffles with more apple skin, or a pinch of finely ground fennel seeds, or one whole toasted fennel seed.

Makes 20 to 25 truffles

1 cup/260 g ganache (page 25)

2½ tablespoons/30 g apple brandy

1 teaspoon/2 g ground toasted fennel seeds

Garnish: apple skin powder (see headnote) and/or fennel pollen

1. Place all the ingredients, except the garnish, in a medium-size bowl and stir together until emulsified.
2. Taste and adjust the flavor as necessary—though be aware that the more liqueur is added, the softer and more difficult to work with the ganache will be.
3. Form into truffles as directed in the Truffles Master Recipe (page 31). Drop each truffle after dipping into a shallow container of apple skin powder, then garnish liberally with fennel pollen, or use only one or the other, as desired.

pomegranate truffles

Pomegranate Truffles! Uncomplicated. Not so sweet. Nice and tart. Pretty. You'll like 'em. I've been making this truffle since I was in my early twenties, lifetimes ago.

PomTrufs' goodness and workaday tastiness negate the tough everyday bitter-pill stuff that is fussy caramel or a president who brings shame to your country. Pomegranate Truffles are a hopeful truffle, a puppy wiggling in your lap. This is one of the ones you're going to snack on a lot as you're piping it. You can pour this ganache into a crisp baked tart shell and slice it into tiny wedges and feed those wedges to people who think vegan desserts are gross and watch their faces change in interesting ways that give you secret pleasure on many levels.

This truffle is garnished with a rose petal, and maybe because of guilt for using a ready-made product to flavor the truffle, the little rose petal garnish occupies more of my brain than it should.

Makes 20 to 25 truffles

1 cup/260 g ganache (page 25)

2 tablespoons/32 g pomegranate molasses

Garnish: fresh or dried rose petals, preferably organically grown (optional)

1. Place all the ingredients, except the garnish, in a medium-size bowl and stir together until emulsified.
2. Taste and adjust the flavor as necessary.
3. Form into truffles as directed in the Truffles Master Recipe (page 31).
4. If desired, garnish the truffles with rose petals—just one or two per truffle, otherwise it gets over-whelming.

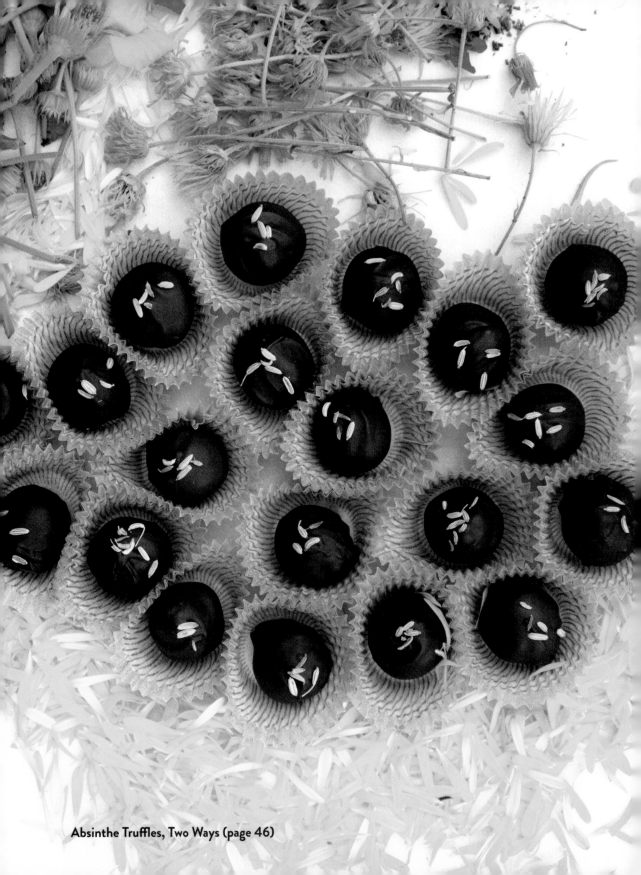

Absinthe Truffles, Two Ways (page 46)

Boozy Truffles

Boozy truffles aren't a gimmick, they're just good. Alcohol and ganache are natural pals, each flavor raises up the other. Alcohol, like fruit, can make ganache too soft to pipe and roll, so, you know—moderation. The easiest way to make all the truffles in this section is just to take some ganache, add some alcohol to taste, and roll them into truffles. The following recipes have proportions that work for us, and some include ideas for another technique that creates a more concentrated boozy flavor: alcohol syrups.

Knowing how to make a quick alcohol reduction syrup is a good skill to have. A boozy syrup can perk up a glass of fizzy water without adding too much alcohol, can garnish a dish made with a splash of that spirit real nicely, and can be used in chocolate making and confectionery in all kinds of ways.

My general rule for boozy truffles is to use the nicest, most expensive alcohol you can when mixing it into ganache straight up, and to use the second-cheapest alcohol in the wine shop when making a reduction. I've experimented with all kinds of alcohols to use for truffles, primarily port, since our Port-Walnut Truffles are a best seller. The cheapest port you can buy makes an acrid, cloying syrup, but an expensive port loses most of its nuances and character in the saucepan. Get one on the second shelf up from the floor.

absinthe truffles, two ways

I'd been making absinthe truffles illegally for years for pals, using a bottle a friend smuggled back from Europe. When this weird, strong, anise-scented liqueur became legal in the United States, we started selling them in the shop. Now we buy superfancy locally made absinthe from a woman you have to meet in a supermarket parking lot for the trade. She signs each bottle.

To really emphasize the fennel note in absinthe, the following syrup recipe includes fennel seeds, which add another layer of mysterious and savory flavor.

You can combine this recipe with the Fennel-Apple Skin Truffles recipe (page 40); and it makes a supremely rad truffle, lots and lots of good flavors happening.

Makes 20 to 25 truffles

Method #1: Full-Strength Alcohol

1 cup/260 g ganache (page 25)

2 tablespoons/25 g absinthe

Garnish: whole or cracked fennel seeds, or fennel pollen

1. Place all the ingredients in a medium-size bowl and stir together until emulsified.
2. Taste and adjust the flavor as necessary.
3. Form into truffles as directed in the Truffles Master Recipe (page 31). Garnish with fennel seeds, cracked or whole, or fennel pollen (see Fennel–Apple Skin Truffles [page 40], for information on fennel pollen).

Method #2: Boozy Syrup

~~~~~~

½ cup/116 g absinthe

3 tablespoons/35 g sugar

1 tablespoon/6 g fennel seeds, lightly cracked with a mortar and pestle or
   in a spice grinder, or by running a rolling pin over them

1 cup/260 g ganache (page 25)

Garnish: whole or cracked fennel seeds, or fennel pollen

~~~~~~

1. Make Absinthe-Fennel Syrup: Combine the absinthe, sugar, and fennel seeds in a small saucepan and bring to a boil over medium heat. Simmer gently until reduced to 3 tablespoons. Transfer the syrup to a container as soon as it's reduced, otherwise it will continue to reduce in the hot pan.
2. Combine the ganache with 1 tablespoon plus 1 teaspoon/20 g of the syrup, or to taste. Use the rest of the syrup to flavor drinks or other desserts. Store leftover syrup in the refrigerator, where it will keep for weeks.
3. Taste and adjust the flavor as necessary.
4. Form into truffles as directed in the Truffles Master Recipe (page 31).
5. Garnish with fennel seeds or fennel pollen.

(recipe photo shown on page 44)

coconut-rum truffles

. . . .

I love this hackneyed, mainstreamy truffle. We've been making it for over ten years and there's nothing wrong with it. It tastes good. Make it! Coconut and rum, no shame!

We've found that coconut extract strength can vary widely, so be sure to taste this one a lot as you're making it.

Depending on how much you like coconut, you can roll this truffle in toasted shredded (unsweetened, the health food store kind) coconut or just sprinkle a little on top. Or get big coconut flakes and toast them and put them on top for a more dramatic effect. Be sure to deeply toast your coconut; it really makes it taste like coconut.

I haven't included a recipe for rum syrup here because dark rum is so syrupy and rich already that making a syrup from it actually hurts your cause.

Makes 20 to 25 truffles

1 cup/260 g ganache (page 25)

1½ teaspoons/10 g coconut extract

1 tablespoon plus 1 teaspoon/10 g dark rum

Garnish: toasted coconut (toast at 350°F, stirring and checking every 5 minutes to make
    sure it's not burning, 10 to 15 minutes, or until it's medium-brown and smells fragrant)

1. Place all the ingredients, except the garnish, in a medium-size bowl and stir together until emulsified.
2. Taste and adjust the flavor as necessary.
3. Form into truffles as directed in the Truffles Master Recipe (page 31). Garnish by rolling in coconut or sprinkle a dusting of coconut on the top of the truffle.

kahlúa truffles

····························

Kahlúa is a buttery, coffee-flavored, rum-based liqueur that adds warmth and an aromatic nose to truffles. It's vegan, yep! (I called the company—I know vegans, boy, do I.) Because it's already rich and concentrated, I haven't included a recipe for making a syrup from it. If you are like my mom (cool, fun-loving, perfect in every way), you will want to whisk one or many more than one of these into your afternoon coffee.

Makes 20 to 25 truffles

1 cup/260 g ganache (page 25)
2 tablespoons/30 g Kahlúa
Garnish: espresso beans

1. Place all the ingredients, except the garnish, in a medium-size bowl and stir together until emulsified.
2. Taste and adjust the flavor as necessary.
3. Form into truffles as directed in the Truffles Master Recipe (page 31). Garnish each with a coffee bean.

port-walnut truffles, two ways

· ·

We use a black walnut extract for this truffle, but nocino, a walnut liqueur, makes a spectacular truffle if you don't want to buy a whole bottle of extract just for this recipe (You can make your own nocino from foraged young English walnuts, too. Find a friend with an English walnut tree and give yourself two months for aging.) The combination of the two alcohols lends depth and interest to the truffle.

This is our New York City shop manager Veronica's favorite confection of the hundreds she's tried over the past ten years of being in the LL-verse. It's a sturdy and elegant truffle, interesting and stylish, like Vern.

Makes 20 to 25 truffles

Method #1: Full-Strength Alcohol

1 cup/260 g ganache (page 25)

1 tablespoon/10 g tawny port (ruby port is just fine, too, just a little sweeter)

½ teaspoon/1 g black walnut extract, or 2 teaspoons/3 g nocino

1. Place all the ingredients in a medium-size bowl and stir together until emulsified.
2. Taste and adjust the flavor as necessary.
3. Form into truffles as directed in the Truffles Master Recipe (page 31).
4. This truffle has no garnish! We just do a little swoop on top when setting it on the pan. Simplicity.

Method #2: Boozy Syrup

If you don't have nocino, just make up the difference with more port. Everyone at our shop thinks this truffle tastes super Christmassy. It's pretty great, dressy and fancy-feeling.

~~~~~~

1 cup/235 g tawny port

1 cup/235 g nocino

1 cup/260 g ganache (page 25)

~~~~~~

1. Make Port-Nocino Syrup: Combine the port and nocino a small saucepan and bring to a boil in over medium heat. Simmer gently until reduced to ¼ cup. Remove from the heat as soon as the syrup is reduced, otherwise it will continue to reduce in the pot.
2. Combine the ganache with 1 tablespoon plus 1 teaspoon/20 g of the syrup. Store leftover syrup in the refrigerator, where it will keep for weeks.
3. Taste and adjust the flavor as necessary.
4. Form into truffles as directed in the Truffles Master Recipe (page 31).
5. Garnish with a loop of chocolate from the dipping fork when setting the truffles on a parchment-covered sheet pan.

Spicy and Strange Truffles

I don't love sweet sweets. I want to push candy as far toward lunch as it will go. These flavor profiles aren't that weird once you taste them, though—they match chocolate's own lush, deep savory notes perfectly. Think of them as less sweet sweets, and they aren't scary at all.

We've had success with caramels with savory elements, particularly salt and spice, but when I have a truly weird ingredient to mess around with, my hands always start whisking up ganache. Dark chocolate ganache seems to want strangeness. The lower sugar content of ganache compared with caramels plays better with umami-rich and fatty ingredients, and the silky texture of a truffle is a good foil to the good shock of salt or vegetal flavors.

Practically, risky savory ganaches are easier than caramels because they're simpler and adjustable. To go rogue with caramel, you have to cook a batch to a precise temperature and let it cool before learning how your experiment turned out. Ganache is friendlier: just keep adding your weird ingredient until you like the taste, then form your ganache into truffles.

The truffles in this section live or die on a razor's edge: balance is key. Sometimes the difference between a bowl of chocolate goop and a cool modern-tasting truffle is the slightest pinch of flavoring. Taste often.

beet-coriander truffles

I bet you think I'm going to make you cook beets and smoosh them up into ganache. Nope!

This truffle is simple. Coriander gives it a beautiful citrus-nutty-woodsy flavor, and the beet garnish is almost completely for color, adding only a small amount of earthiness.

I'm old now and I've been in therapy for perfectionistic tendencies for a while, so if you buy those vegetable chips made of beets and crumble them up to use in this truffle, I applaud you. Or do what we do: slice raw beets with a mandoline set as thin as you can stand or slice as thinly as you can, then dry in a dehydrator set to around 110°F overnight or an oven turned as low as you can, until they're completely dried out but not browned at all (an hour or so, but watch carefully for browning). Grind in a spice grinder or mortar and pestle to make a fine powder with some small chunks left for personality. Store in an airtight container at room temperature for several months.

Be sure to toast the coriander seeds: toasting maximizes the flavor and it only takes a second. Grind them in the same unwashed spice grinder or mortar and pestle you used for the beets. Or get fancy and use a mortar and pestle to crush them.

Makes 20 to 25 truffles

1 cup/260 g ganache (page 25)
1 tablespoon/4 g coriander powder, made from freshly toasted, ground coriander seeds
Garnish: beet powder (see headnote)

1. Place all the ingredients, except the garnish, in a medium-size bowl and stir together until emulsified.
2. Taste and adjust the flavor as necessary.
3. Form into truffles as directed in the Truffles Master Recipe (page 31).
4. Sprinkle a little beet powder on top of the wet, freshly dipped truffles.

(recipe photo shown on page 27)

chipotle and caramelized onion truffles

All hail Chipotle and Caramelized Onion, queen of the unexpected. The most complicated truffle we make, and still not all that complicated. The keys here are to grind the onions until they are a puree, with no onion chunks, and to add just enough of the onion. Too little and people will feel like they missed out on something great. Too much and it's too much.

For a garnish, we shave chocolate into big spiky chunks so it's visually and texturally disorienting, too. Afflict the comfortable, comfort the afflicted, all that.

This truffle, like most dishes made with chiles, has the interesting effect of a delayed heat reaction. First, you taste chocolate ganache, then a slightly oniony undertone, then a mix of the two, then, a little down the line, just when you were beginning to feel disappointed, the chipotle flavor appears. Some Willy Wonka stuff there, I know. Chiles are so cool.

Makes 20 to 25 truffles

1 cup/260 g ganache (page 25)

1 teaspoon/4 g chipotle powder, or to taste

2¼ teaspoons/13 g caramelized onion (recipe follows), pureed to a paste in a
    food processor or blender or chopped very, very, very finely

Garnish: shaved chocolate curls (see directions)

1. Place all the ingredients, except the garnish, in a medium-size bowl and stir together until emulsified.
2. Taste and adjust the flavors as necessary.
3. Form into truffles as directed in the Truffles Master Recipe (page 31).
4. To make chocolate curls for a garnish, use a vegetable peeler to shave pieces off a large hunk of dark chocolate.
5. Drop the dipped truffles onto the bed of chocolate curls, then roll them around a little in the chocolate for a spiky look.

Caramelized Onions That Will Change Your Whole Life

Once you know how to make real-deal caramelized onions, your life is pretty much set. All your friends will like you more, potential lovers you want to woo will be appropriately wooed, enemies you made before you started going to therapy will flip back to the friend side of things, everyone who's ever unfriended you will re-friend you. Caramelized onions make everything better. They aren't hard to make, I don't know why everyone isn't constantly making them at all times.

When I worked at Bloodroot in Connecticut, where 99 percent of all dishes are onion-based, the residing matriarch and my eventual best friend Selma said that the only real way not to tear up when chopping onions is to put the very first onion slice, a thin sliver cut off the tip before peeling, on your head. Use your hair to anchor it and keep it there while chopping. I never remember to do this until I'm halfway in and already crying, but the few times I have it's always worked. Selma said it was about moving the onion above your eyes. It's an open secret that everything about Bloodroot is shot through with a sort of witchy wild woman magic that I'd usually make fun of, but in Bloodroot's case I'm completely convinced/charmed. Try the onion thing.

1. Peel some onions. Cut in half stem to root, not along the equator. Thinly slice following the grain of the onion, stem to root again. Throw out the nubbly, hairy root part.
2. Pour a few glugs of extra-virgin olive oil—nothing superfancy—into a large, wide, straight-sided pan. Add a nice big pinch of salt and cook everything over medium-low-ish heat, stirring every few minutes, for 20 minutes or so, until the onions start to get lightly browned. Lower the heat a bit if this seems to be going too fast. If they start sticking to the pan, put the lid on for a few minutes or deglaze by tossing in some water, wine, brandy, vegetable stock or broth, or pretty much any other liquid, just enough to keep everything moist and moving. Keep cooking for another 10 or 15 minutes, or until everything is golden brown, a.k.a. "caramelized." If you like to really push things, let them get superbrowned and crackly.

ginger — orange blossom truffles

....

Orange flower water is a delicate flavoring that can be hard to taste over the intense flavor of ganache. Adding a little ginger brings out both flavors. You can quickly make ginger juice by rubbing peeled ginger over a ginger grater or Microplane zester, then squeezing the pulp until you have enough juice. Or you can buy it bottled in health food stores.

Years ago, when she worked at the chocolate shop; this truffle was my best friend Maresa's favorite confection. The first time I made it, she closed her eyes while eating it and softly said, "This is the best thing we've ever made."

Makes 20 to 25 truffles

1 cup/260 g ganache (page 25)

2 teaspoons/10 g ginger juice

1½ tablespoons/17 g orange flower water

½ teaspoon/2 g culinary-grade orange oil (not extract or essential oil)

Garnish: crystallized ginger, cut into tidy little squares or wands

1. Place all the ingredients, except the garnish, in a medium-size bowl and stir together until emulsified.
2. Taste and adjust the flavor as necessary.
3. Form into truffles as directed in the Truffles Master Recipe (page 31).
4. Press a little bit of crystallized ginger onto each truffle right after you dip it. Use your fingertip to grab a tiny bit of wet chocolate from the truffle and fold it over the ginger piece, to make a seatbelt for it.

harissa truffles

· ·

Harissa is a Tunisian pepper mixture. It's medium-spicy—gentler than the chipotle-onion truffle, but still plenty hot. Like the chipotle truffle, its heat arrives slowly, allowing you to taste the other flavors in the harissa first.

If you don't want to mix up your own harissa powder (recipe follows), plenty of ready-made versions exist. The leftover powder can be sprinkled on roasting potatoes, grilled peppers, chickpea dishes—it makes most food more complex and interesting. You can also blend it with olive oil and dried mild chiles to make a paste that keeps for weeks in the refrigerator and is many times better than the sum of its parts.

Unlike caramelized onions or truffle mushrooms, the amount of harissa you put in your ganache is a matter of personal preference—a little less and you'll have a very nice truffle subtly flavored with spice; a little more and you'll have a spicy, extra-vibrant truffle. This is a hard one to mess up.

Makes 20 to 25 truffles

1 cup/260 g ganache (page 25)
1½ tablespoons/10 g harissa powder, or to taste
Garnish: harissa powder (recipe follows)

1. Place all the ingredients, except the garnish, in a medium-size bowl and stir together until emulsified.
2. Taste and adjust the flavor as necessary.
3. Form into truffles as directed in the Truffles Master Recipe (page 31).
4. Garnish with a little harissa powder.

Harissa Powder

3 tablespoons/23 g dried ground chiles (use whatever chiles you like; we use
    medium-spicy Aleppo peppers, but ancho or chipotle powders are nice, too)
1 tablespoon/7 g whole cumin seeds
2 tablespoons/14 g whole coriander seeds
1 tablespoon/7 g whole caraway seeds

1. Put all the spices in a dry saucepan and toast over medium heat, stirring constantly, until one shade darker and fragrant (about 5 minutes). Remove from the heat and let cool.
2. Grind in a spice grinder, food processor, or mortar and pestle—don't worry about making a super-uniform powder, some small chunks and bits of spice give this truffle an interesting texture and flavor.
3. To make this powder into a spicy paste (homemade hot sauce!) that will keep in your refrigerator for weeks, whisk it with olive oil, a little red wine vinegar, and salt and pepper to taste.

shiitake sea salt double truffles

··

The Double Truffle: so nice, we named it twice. A truffle made with truffle mushrooms. And shiitake mushrooms, too, because a truffle flavored with just truffle mushrooms would be overpoweringly earthy, and a truffle flavored with just shiitake mushrooms is hard to taste without adding so much shiitake powder that the texture suffers. Together, they sing.

Because my life's mission is to make vegan food that's meatier than meat and brings all meat-eaters simpering to their knees in want of it, I use a lot of mushrooms. They're a lazy trick to signify meatiness.

Log-grown shiitake are worlds away from typical industrial sawdust-grown mushrooms, thick and juicy, oozing earth and meat. But if you can't get log-grown, this recipe will work with whatever kind of shiitakes you can get your hands on.

You can use a little truffle oil to flavor the ganache, but most truffle oils aren't actually distilled from truffles—they're mostly artificial flavors permeating low-quality oils. To add a real truffle flavor, we use truffle-infused salt. Try to smell the truffle salt before you buy it. A good one will knock you out with a distinct, earthy truffle smell as soon as you open the container.

To make shiitake powder, stem some shiitake mushrooms and dry in a low oven until crispy (set the oven on the lowest setting and bake for thirty minutes to an hour, watching closely for burning), then let cool, grind to a powder in a coffee grinder, and strain through a fine strainer. Or buy dried shiitake mushrooms in a health food store or Asian market. At Asian markets, look for thick ones that are expensive, crispy, light, and have a crackled cap, often labeled "donko."

Makes 20 to 25 truffles

1 cup/260 g ganache (page 25)

¾ teaspoon/2 g sea salt or truffle-infused sea salt, or to taste

1 tablespoon plus 1 teaspoon/4 g shiitake powder, or to taste

½ pound chocolate, for dipping

Garnish: truffle-infused sea salt

1. Place all the ingredients, except the garnish, in a medium-size bowl and stir together until emulsified.
2. Taste and adjust the flavor as necessary.
3. Form into truffles as directed in the Truffles Master Recipe (page 31).
4. Garnish with a little truffle-infused sea salt.

white miso truffles

Miso is a special food for me. Over fifteen years ago, Sandor Katz's brilliant book *Wild Fermentation* opened up a universe of fermenting fun in my cooking life. Immediately after reading it, I started (1) making miso, and (2) angling to befriend Sandor. I've done both and my life is perfect now. Sandor is a gem of a human, and miso making makes life extra sparkly. Homemade miso takes months or years, but if you don't want to start a batch of your own (do it!), any tasty store-bought miso will work in this recipe. I like to use the lighter misos, such as chickpea, brown rice, or anything labeled "white" or "shiro" miso. Red misos and other darker, more aged misos will make a more intense truffle, so you might want to use a little less. Let your taste buds be your guideline. South River Miso is a great, tasty, widely-available brand. If you're a salt pal, garnish this truffle (also everything) with one of those pricey flaky gorgeous sea salts that are pretty and add a layer of crunch and extra layer of good salt flavor to these. Or release a flotilla of cocoa powder over the wet truffles to add explosions of bitterness on top of deep salty miso—astonishingly good, an unsweet sweet, you feel un-American eating it, sorta traitorous to birthday cake and those cupcakes with tiny doughnuts stuck onto them at jaunty angles.

Makes 20 to 25 truffles

1 cup/260 g ganache (page 25)
1 tablespoon/19 g white miso, or to taste
Garnish: unsweetened cocoa powder

1. Place the miso in a medium-size bowl and mix with a little ganache.
2. Combine the miso mixture with the remaining ganache. Stir until emulsified.
3. Taste and adjust the flavor as necessary.
4. Form into truffles as directed in the Truffles Master Recipe (page 31).
5. Spoon a little cocoa powder over each truffle.

GANACHE FILLINGS, FROSTINGS, AND SAUCES

Ganache does a bang-up job turning into things other than truffles. Here are some frostings, fillings, dips, sauces, and drinks that make use of everyone's favorite fat-in-water emulsion.

First, a cake and two frostings to top it with.

Poured Ganache Frosting (page 75)

chocolate cake

. . . .

I love this chocolate cake. I don't even like chocolate cake. But it's a good, solid, friendly one. This recipe is adapted to the point of utter unrecognizability from *The Voluptuous Vegan*, a cookbook by one of my culinary school instructors, Myra Kornfeld, a warm, kind teacher who loves food and makes you love it, too. Myra is one of those strangely cuddly New Yorkers, an Upper West Side kind of person who takes pleasure in things being just-so in an exciting, not fussy, way.

This cake never fails. During the decade I worked as a private chef and ran a meal delivery service, I churned out endless variations of it. (Spicy chocolate cake! Superspicy chocolate cake! German chocolate cake! Spelt chocolate cake! Black Forest chocolate cake! Peanut butter chocolate cake!). My two dented (they're always dented; do they come dented?) glass-bottomed springform pans were in constant rotation.

The absolute easiest way to mix up a cake: wet bowl, dry bowl, and done. You do need a really big bowl, though. And be sure not to forget to mix the water into the dry ingredients—it gives the cake structure. This cake isn't too sweet. Wrapped tightly in plastic wrap, the cake layers will keep, unfrosted, for five days in the refrigerator.

Makes one double-layer or two single-layer 9-inch cakes

1 cup/100 g unsweetened cocoa powder, plus more for dusting (optional)

2 cups/400 g organic evaporated cane juice sugar

3 cups/450 g all-purpose flour, plus more for dusting (optional)

1 teaspoon/5 g baking soda

4 teaspoons/10 g baking powder

1 teaspoon/7 g sea salt

2 tablespoons/10 g ground coffee, ideally freshly ground

1¾ cups/400 g water

1¼ cups/300 g canned full-fat coconut milk, warmed to emulsify if necessary

1 tablespoon/15 g apple cider vinegar

¾ cup/140 g olive oil

2 teaspoons/10 g pure vanilla extract

1. Preheat the oven to 350°F.
2. Oil two 9-inch round pans (springform ones with removable bottoms are best). Dust a little flour or cocoa powder onto the pans.
3. Sift the dry ingredients into a large bowl. Stir the water into the dry ingredients.
4. Mix together the wet ingredients in a medium-size bowl.
5. Add the wet mixture to the dry mixture and stir just until combined. Don't overmix, or your cake will be tough. Immediately pour into the prepared pans, dividing the batter evenly between the pans.
6. Bake for 30 to 40 minutes, or until the middle is no longer jiggly, a cake tester inserted into the center of each cake comes out clean, and the cake pulls from the sides of the pan slightly.
7. Remove from the oven and let cool on a wire rack in the pan for a few minutes, then turn the rack over the pan and invert to remove the cake from the pan. Let the cake cool completely before frosting.
8. If you'd like a perfectly level surface to frost, use a serrated knife to level off the tops (making lots of cake scraps for nibbling), then flip the cakes over before frosting. Or just frost them as is, in single layers, for two domed cakes.

Two Similar Frostings

These frostings have pretty much the same ingredients but in slightly different configurations, which create completely different effects on cakes. They can be flavored with ingredients stolen from any truffle flavors mentioned earlier, and garnished similarly to how the truffles are garnished.

I love and constantly desire big puffed-up frosting roses, scripty words on cakes, and those Instagrammy big messy cakes with piles of cookies and macarons, meringue, shards of spiky chocolate, crunchies and brittles and feuilletine heaped on top—I love it all. But ganache-frosted cakes are the Eileen Fisher of baked goods: simple, interesting, well made but not show-offy. They gracefully eschew excess ornament, confident of their intrinsic worth. I dress nothing like someone who shops at Eileen Fisher (100 percent of this book advance is going to vintage stretchy Betsey Johnson wiggle dresses), but I'm super restrained with these kinds of cakes. They're hugely rich, and they already look so good. They don't need garnish piles or frosting flowers. They're not very sweet at all.

Here are a few super simple ideas for dressing up ganache-frosted cakes post frosting without overwhelming them or inducing a huge sugar headache in the people who eat them:

- Sprinkle liberally with flaky sea salt. Do this! Ganache and fancy salt. Yes.
- Strew a few dried or fresh flower petals on top.
- Set some good local berries or other fruit on top.
- Sift a little cocoa powder or confectioners' sugar over the whole cake, or set a piece of paper on top of it and sift cocoa powder or confectioners' sugar over half of the cake, then remove the paper to create a nice sharp line.
- Set a paper doily on top and sift cocoa powder or confectioners' sugar over it, then carefully lift it off.
- Drag a decorating comb or other scalloped or interestingly shaped object across the ganache to make a cool pattern.
- Shave some dark chocolate onto the cake with a Y-shaped peeler.

whipped ganache frosting

· ·

This is a homey fudgy chocolate frosting that works equally well as a filling for your cake of choice. Or make cookie sandwiches with it, parfaits with vegan whipped cream, or frost cookies, doughnuts, brownies, or cupcakes with it. Dip things into it. You get the idea.

This recipe is ultrasimple, but also pretty temperature sensitive. If you're working in a hot room, you'll want to use the frosting when it's somewhat cold. Return it to the refrigerator as needed to firm it up. If you don't have a standing mixer, use a handheld mixer, or whisk it like crazy with a wire whisk.

Makes enough to frost one 9-inch double-layer cake

1¼ cups/270 g coconut milk

1½ tablespoons/18 g coconut oil

12 ounces (2¼ cups)/345 g bittersweet chocolate, chopped into small pieces

2 tablespoons/25 g brandy or other alcohol

¼ teaspoon/2 g sea salt

1. Combine the milk and oil with 3 tablespoons of water in a 2-quart pot and bring to a boil, then remove from the heat and add the remaining ingredients. Cover and let sit a few minutes. Gently whisk to emulsify.
2. Let sit in the refrigerator until set up, stirring every 10 minutes or so, about 45 minutes, or until just cooled.
3. Transfer to a standing mixer fitted with a whisk attachment and whip on medium speed just until light and fluffy, adding up to 4 tablespoons more water to make a light fluffy consistency. The frosting will become grainy if overwhipped.
4. Set one cake layer on an inverted plate or revolving cake decorating stand. Fill with roughly one quarter of the frosting, spreading evenly to the edges. Or fill with thinned-out jam, another

flavor of frosting, or your choice of filling. Transfer the second cake layer on top, making sure the upside-down, supereven base of that layer is facing upward.

5.   Use a small amount of frosting to cover the cake with only a very thin layer of frosting. Refrigerate the cake for 30 minutes or so, to ensure a nice, firm surface for the final frosting layer. You can skip this step, but colder cakes are nicer to frost.

6.   If your frosting has set up and is too hard to spread, rewhip it in the standing mixer with another tablespoon of water. Using an offset spatula, frost the cake with big swoopy swirls of frosting by pressing the spatula downward into the frosting and lifting it up slightly to make a fluffy swoop.

poured ganache frosting

· ·

This frosting is for pouring (surprise!) over cakes, cupcakes, petits fours, doughnuts, or brownies. It makes a matte, mega-chocolaty, lush frosting that cuts beautifully with gorgeous clean lines that look stylish and put together. If you want to garnish your cake with what is basically a flat truffle, here you go.

Makes enough to frost one 9-inch double-layer cake

1¼ cups/260 g coconut milk

1½ tablespoons/18 g coconut oil

12 ounces/2½ cups/345 g bittersweet chocolate, chopped into small pieces

2 tablespoons/24 g brandy or other alcohol

¼ teaspoon/2 g sea salt

1. Set one layer of a 9-inch or smaller cake on a raised wire rack on a half sheet pan (18 by 13 inches) lined with waxed paper or parchment paper.
2. Bring the milk to a boil in a 2-quart pot, then remove from the heat and add the remaining ingredients. Cover and let sit a few minutes. Gently whisk to emulsify. Pour into a 4-cup measuring cup or other container with a pouring spout. (Or just pour it from the pot; no fear, go for it!)
3. Spoon roughly one quarter of the frosting over the first layer, spreading evenly to edges. Or fill with thinned-out jam, another flavor of frosting, or your choice of filling. Transfer the second cake layer on top, making sure the upside-down, supereven base of the layer is facing upward.
4. Optional: use a small amount of frosting to cover the cake with only a very thin layer of frosting. Let sit for 10 minutes to firm up.
5. Pour half of the remaining frosting evenly over the cake. Let rest for 5 minutes, then pour the rest over the cake, making sure to pour it over any naked spots from the initial pour.
6. If the frosting sets up too quickly and isn't pourable, gently warm it in a microwave on low power or over a double boiler.

(recipe photo shown on page 68)

five-minute chocolate sauce

· ·

I don't really have to explain what chocolate sauce is, unless you're European or something. Drizzle it on things. Okay.

This is a cheater's chocolate sauce, not true chocolate fudge. In exchange for a sauce that is slightly less satiny and glossy than a "real" fudge sauce, you save the hassle of fiddling with a candy thermometer and watching a boiling pot for half an hour. This sauce keeps in the fridge for several weeks, where it will become firm and ganachelike and will need warming in a microwave or double boiler to become fluid again.

Makes 2 cups sauce

1 cup/240 g coconut milk
2 tablespoons/30 g water
½ cup/200 g Cane Syrup (page 96) or organic corn syrup
2 cups/310 g bittersweet chocolate, finely chopped

1. Combine the milk, water, and syrup in a 2-quart pot and bring to a low boil, stirring often.
2. Add the chocolate and whisk to combine. Cook for 2 minutes, or until glossy and smooth, then remove from the heat and let cool.

chocolate syrup

. . . .

Thin out your chocolate sauce with a little more cane syrup (see page 96), and it's now chocolate syrup. It keeps months in the freezer and weeks in the refrigerator.

egg creams

. . . .

Add a spoonful of chocolate syrup to a tall glass with some almond or other nondairy milk, add some seltzer and ice (proportions are up to you), and you've made a real authentic (okay, sort of authentic) New York egg cream. Egg creams never use eggs or cream, because if there's one place on earth that can hold many contradictions in its heart at once, it's New York City. Enjoy!

Classic Drinking Chocolate (page 80)

DRINKING CHOCOLATE

This is not your childhood powdery hot cocoa. True European-style drinking chocolates—not American-style thin, sweet hot chocolate—use astonishingly huge quantities of chocolate: a full quarter-cup of ganache, equivalent to five truffles. You can make this recipe lighter, though. Because I run a vegan chocolate shop and am obsessed with hitting people over the head with the idea that vegan food doesn't have to be boring and puritanical, our Drinking Chocolate is about as fatty as we can make it. Maybe you won't have such a chip on your shoulder and will modify our recipe to your taste accordingly.

We use sweetened, boxed, organic, vanilla-flavored almond milk in our Drinking Chocolates, but you can use any milk. For customers who can't have nuts, we use canned coconut milk, and it's an even richer, glossier, bonkersier drink. If you're the sort of person who likes to make your own nut milks, use them. If you're the sort of person who likes to make your own nut milks you probably don't need a recipe for them, so I won't provide one.

One way to make these drinks a little lighter is to use water instead of almond milk. Our chocolate shop head manager Kate calls that option "Divorce Cocoa" because it smacks, just a little, of sadness and a sparse pantry. I don't mind it at all, though—water Drinking Chocolate has a purity and a chocolate-forward flavor I like a lot. On the other hand, I grew up fervently wishing my parents would get a divorce.

We garnish our Drinking Chocolates with homemade coconut-based whipped cream, vegan marshmallows, and coarsely ground canela cinnamon. Canela is also sold as "Mexican cinnamon," and you can get it in Mexican markets. It's really nice and crumbly. Any other kind of cinnamon works, too.

classic drinking chocolate

· ·

Makes 6 ounces drinking chocolate

½ cup plus 1 tablespoon/140 g milk of choice (we prefer slightly sweetened almond milk)

1½ teaspoons/7 g sugar

¼ cup/45 to 50 g ganache (page 25), or to taste

Vegan marshmallows

Coarsely ground cinnamon

Lagusta's Luscious Whipped Cream (page 84)

1. Combine the milk and sugar in a small saucepan and heat over medium heat until simmering.
2. Lower the heat to low and whisk in the ganache. Whisk until emulsified.
3. Remove from the heat. Pour into a mug, then garnish with marshmallows, cinnamon, and Lagusta's Luscious Whipped Cream.

(recipe photo shown on page 78)

tot chocolate

Tot Chocolate, adorably named by my friend Tara Tornello, is for kids who will ruin the lives of nearby adult people after consuming a full cup of Drinking Chocolate, and for any human who might want to eat a meal at some point afterward. It's just Drinking Chocolate with a little less ganache and a little more milk.

Makes 6 ounces Tot Chocolate

½ cup plus 1 tablespoon/150 g milk of choice (we prefer slightly sweetened almond milk)

1½ tablespoons sugar

3 tablespoons/35 g ganache (page 25), or to taste

Vegan marshmallows

Coarsely ground cinnamon

Lagusta's Luscious Whipped Cream (page 84)

1. Combine the milk and sugar in a small saucepan and heat over medium heat until simmering.
2. Lower the heat to low and whisk in the ganache. Whisk until emulsified.
3. Remove from the heat. Pour into a mug, then garnish with marshmallows, cinnamon, and Lagusta's Luscious Whipped Cream.

spicy drinking chocolate

· ·

Mix three parts ground mild chiles, such as ancho chile powder, with one part spicy chiles, such as chipotle powder, and add as desired to your Drinking Chocolate while heating the milk. We use ¼ to ½ teaspoon per Drinking Chocolate, depending on how spicy the customer wants their drink. Sprinkle a little of the spicy mixture on top of the whipped cream instead of or in addition to the cinnamon, for another jolt of good chile flavor.

caffé cacao

· ·

Coffee and chocolate, ultimate pals of the universe, a buddy movie of highest-grossing box office receipts, killer opening weekend, spawning slash fiction aplenty. Each elevates the other, they've got all their in-jokes, their pleasure in each other's company palpable. Caffé Cacao is our fancy way of making an inverted mocha, more chocolate than coffee.

Makes 7 ounces Caffé Cacao

½ cup plus 1 tablespoon/140 g milk of choice (we prefer slightly sweetened almond milk)

1½ teaspoons/6 g sugar

¼ cup/45–50 g ganache (page 25), or to taste

2 tablespoons/20 g coffee concentrate (recipe follows)

Vegan marshmallows

Coarsely ground cinnamon

Lagusta's Luscious Whipped Cream (page 84)

1. Place the milk and sugar in a small saucepan and heat over medium heat until simmering.
2. Lower the heat to low and whisk in the ganache. Whisk until emulsified. Add the coffee concentrate and heat just to warm, don't boil.
3. Remove from the heat. Pour into a mug, then garnish with marshmallows, cinnamon, and Lagusta's Luscious Whipped Cream.

•────•────•────•

Coffee Concentrate

Coffee concentrate is a sort of magic trick. It's easy, keeps forever, and means you're never far from good iced coffee, Drinking Chocolate spiked with good coffee flavor, or even hot coffee. It makes an amazing iced coffee—just dilute with water to taste, a tablespoon or two per glass. For hot coffee, just boil water and add coffee concentrate to taste, roughly two parts water to one part concentrate. This is a good way to make coffee quickly for a party, especially if you typically make pour-over coffee at home and making one cup of coffee takes five minutes of lovingly careful hot water dripping, which doesn't work well for a crowd unless you like people staring at you for a long time. Using coffee concentrate to make hot coffee is cheating and I don't care.

Go for nice, ethically procured single-origin coffee beans, which make an extra-sparkly concentrate—since the concentrated is never heated, you taste the full complexity of the beans.

Coffee concentrate keeps for weeks in the refrigerator and freezes beautifully, but halving the recipe works just as well.

Makes about 2 cups concentrate

6 ounces/170 g coffee beans, coarsely ground
3¾ cups/875 g cold filtered water

1. Pour the beans into 2-quart or similar container. Add the water and stir gently to ensure all the grounds are saturated with the water.
2. Cover and let sit at room temperature for 24 hours. Strain through a coffee filter.

Lagusta's Luscious whipped cream, two ways

....

Whipped Cream for Cream Whip Canisters

I have been obsessively tinkering with whipped cream for over a decade. Twice a year or so, I overhaul our whip, because I think it can be better. I've definitely made it worse many times over. But this is the best incarnation.

What would it be like to not be vegan, to take cream, and whip it—singing you-know-what song even—and be done with the whole business? I work so hard to make a neutral-tasting whip, a whip that tastes like whipped cream. But whipped cream just tastes like dairy. So, why can't I make whipped cream that tastes like coconut without being a failure as a vegan chef? Why is the default flavor always milk? These are questions for another day. This whip doesn't taste too much like coconut due to a massive dose of vanilla extract.

Use full-fat canned coconut milk for this. It has the least ingredients (coconut, water, sometimes a touch of guar gum to stabilize) and the best flavor. Aseptic-packed coconut milk won't have a great flavor, and low-fat whipped cream is just depressing for everyone, plus it won't function the same, you'll have a foamy, watery heap instead of a rich, lathery cream.

The trick to this recipe is to make sure you get some semblance of a balance between the firm coconut solids that rise to the top of the can and the watery coconut milk at the bottom of the can. Aim for at least 100 g (about 3.5 ounces) of that nice waxy fat layer. You can be fussy and heat your can and whisk it together before measuring, but we never do.

This whip is more substantial and creamy when allowed to sit, postcharging, in the canister for a day or two. If you have the time, let it hang out a little before using. If it seems thin when first dispensed, wait a day and it should thicken up.

Makes 2 cups whipped cream

2 cups/505 g canned full-fat coconut milk (at least 100 g fat)

½ teaspoon/3 g Genutine or agar powder

⅛ teaspoon/1 g sea salt

¼ cup/30 g confectioners' sugar

2 tablespoons/20 g pure vanilla extract

1 vanilla bean, split and scraped

1. Combine the milk and Genutine in a 2-quart pot and quickly heat over high heat, whisking constantly, until the milk is thickened and almost boiling. Add the salt and confectioners' sugar.
2. Remove from the heat, add the vanilla and vanilla bean scrapings, and transfer to a blender. Blend for about 2 minutes. Chill in the refrigerator at least an hour. If the mixture seems separated after chilling, whisk to emulsify or blend again.
3. Transfer the mixture to a cream whip canister and charge via the manufacturer's instructions with two nitrous oxide chargers, one after another.
4. Shake the canister vigorously after each charge. Shake before using it each time, and dispense cream at an extreme 90-degree angle, with your hand angled back toward the inside of your wrist.

Coconut-Almond Whipped Cream

Lacking an expensive cream whipper gadget, this recipe makes a more substantial whipped cream. It's heavier than the version made for a cream whip canister. Dollop it from a spoon or pipe from a pastry bag. This whipped cream is soft and puddinglike after being processed, then thickens up nicely after chilling in the refrigerator for thirty minutes or so.

If you don't have almond milk and coconut milk, you can use all of one or the other. The combination ensures a satiny texture without an overly coconutty flavor, but just one is just fine.

Makes 1½ cups whipped cream

⅔ cup/170 g almond milk

⅔ cup/170 g canned full-fat coconut milk, plus 2 tablespoons/30 g fatty coconut milk
   from the top of the can

1 teaspoon/4 g agar

7 tablespoons/90 g sugar

¼ teaspoon/2 g sea salt

2 teaspoons/7 g cornstarch, whisked into 2 tablespoons/30 g water

½ teaspoon/1 g xanthan gum

1 tablespoon/10 g pure vanilla extract

½ teaspoon/1 g almond extract

1 teaspoon/4 g freshly squeezed lemon juice

Optional: 1 vanilla bean, split and scraped

1. Combine the almond milk and ⅔ cup/170 g of coconut milk, agar, sugar, and salt in a small sauce-pan and bring to a boil over high heat, whisking often. When the mixture comes to a boil, add the cornstarch slurry and whisk until it returns to a boil. Remove from the heat.
2. Chill in the refrigerator until firm, about 1 hour.
3. Transfer to a food processor and add the remaining ingredients, including the reserved 2 table-spoons/30 g of fatty coconut milk. Process until smooth, scraping down the sides as necessary.
4. If desired, transfer to a piping bag with a star tip. Refrigerate for 30 minutes before using.

frozen drinking chocolate

FDC is

1. One of our best-selling drinks, even in the wintertime
2. Deservedly so
3. A constant stress-maker, what with all the freezing of stuff and fiddly blending instructions
4. A true loss leader, a fancy-francy froufrou beverage that looks suspiciously Starbuxian but is actually as slushily tasty as it looks/truly fulfills the societal expectations such drinks promise and rarely deliver
5. Indistinguishable, veganly speaking, from said bougie beverages, they that are thick with cone-bra caps of whip and cascading ropy swirls of flaxen caramel
6. All of the above

Frozen Drinking Chocolate is not hard to make (unless you're running a business off it). You can keep the mixture in the freezer at all times and be never more than a few minutes from the small-grain crystalline perfection that is FDC.

Be sure not to overblend your mixture. You really only need to blend for thirty seconds or so, depending on how thick the mixture is and how great your blender is. You're going for a slushy texture, not watery.

Cold drinks need more flavor than hot ones to deliver the same intensity, so these proportions are slightly different from the basic Drinking Chocolate. Can you freeze your leftover Drinking Chocolate and blend it into a nice slushy? This anarchist surely isn't going to tell you how to drink your drinks. It'll be lovely. But this is just as easy and better.

Makes 4 or 5 drinks

Frozen Drinking Chocolate Mix

3 cups/700 g almond milk

½ cup/100 g sugar

¾ cup/200 g ganache (page 25)

1. Combine the milk and sugar in a 2-quart pot and heat over medium heat until simmering.
2. Lower the heat to low and whisk in the ganache. Whisk until emulsified.
3. Remove from the heat, let cool for 10 to 15 minutes, then whisk again and freeze in ice cube trays or molds.
4. Once frozen, transfer the frozen cubes to resealable plastic bags and continue to freeze.

To make 1 Frozen Drinking Chocolate:

½ cup/90 g almond milk

1½ cups/200 g Frozen Drinking Chocolate Mix

Basic Caramel Sauce (page 104) (optional)

Five-Minute Chocolate Sauce (page 76) (optional)

Lagusta's Luscious Whipped Cream (page 84)

1. Place the almond milk and Frozen Drinking Chocolate Mix in a blender and blend just until it turns into a thick slushy texture, not until it's completely smooth and watery.
2. Drizzle caramel and/or fudge sauce down the insides of a tall glass. Pour the Frozen Drinking Chocolate into the glass and garnish with whipped cream and more fudge and/or caramel sauce.

Frozen Caffé Cacao

Frozen Caffé Cacao is frankly ridiculous, everything good about this sad old world supernaturally morphed into vital slush form. We make it in our café with espresso, but here's a simpler version with coffee concentrate. If you have readily available espresso, use two shots, but the concentrate makes a more-than-acceptable substitute. Frozen Caffé Cacaos are a little more liquid than the regular Frozen Drinking Chocolates, so take care to blend them in dainty pulses just until they've formed a perfect, velvety slush.

Makes 1 drink

2 tablespoons Coffee Concentrate (page 83)

Scant ½ cup/80 g almond milk

1 cup/160 g Frozen Drinking Chocolate Mix (page 90)

Basic Caramel Sauce (page 104) (optional)

Five-Minute Chocolate Sauce (page 76) (optional)

Lagusta's Luscious Whipped Cream (page 84)

1. Combine the coffee concentrate, milk, and Frozen Drinking Chocolate Mix in a blender and blend just until it's a thick slushy texture, not until it's completely smooth and watery.
2. Drizzle caramel and/or fudge sauce down the insides of a tall glass. Pour the frozen caffé cacao into the glass and garnish with whipped cream and more fudge and/or caramel sauce.

Pumpkin Spice Caramels (page 137)

caramel and the meaning of life

The thing about caramel is that it's sticky. Is that a metaphor, or not? I don't know. It feels like something important. We've stuck together, that's something. If ganache is a sonnet—a small, kinda pretentious thing—caramel is a workaday BFF. Caramel isn't fancy by definition, like ganache. Our caramel is fancy because we add fancy stuff to it, but caramel is still just there, being caramel. Burnt sugar, simple as breathing. You can make caramel sauce by just burning sugar until it liquefies and becomes saucy, and it's great. These recipes have more ingredients to ensure that your caramel confections behave as they should, but they build on a base of just burning sugar.

I'd been making truffles for six years before I started messing with caramel. In 2008, the financial crisis hit and some of my clients for the meal delivery service I ran in Manhattan started dropping off. I used the extra time to lean into caramel, and it took over. In 2010, I debuted my first caramel: the Rosemary Sea Salt Caramel. Sea salt in caramel was still a fairly new thing, which sounds so odd now. Fran's Chocolates in Seattle basically invented the pairing, and now most of our customers come specifically for our sea salt caramels. We have a whole line of them, and the Rosemary Sea Salt Caramel is still the leader of the pack, RSSC a constant presence on our to-do list. I like the Thyme and Preserved Lemon Caramel better, and think of RSSC as our vanilla, as plain as it gets around these parts.

Most of our customers aren't vegans, they're locals who know we make the best confections around. They're our neighbors and friends and community members. But vegans, local and far-away, make a point to seek out our shops in New Paltz and New York City. Good vegan caramel was then and is now almost impossible to find. I don't get why, because making it is identical to making dairy caramel and every vegan on earth craves it. The vegan world is strange like that, sometimes built on economies of scarcity that create frenzied buying sprees fueled on perceived shortages. Works for me!

Our shop has increasingly turned to caramel-based confections because they're cheaper to make (sugar is cheaper than chocolate), have a longer shelf life than most chocolate candies (two months as opposed to two weeks), and we like them better.

Most caramel recipes build on two techniques: **caramel candies** and **caramel sauce**.

For caramel candies, you dump most of your ingredients into the pot at once, bring them to a certain temperature, stirring as little as you can force yourself, then put in some delicate ingredients that aren't heat stable (vanilla extract or any other alcohol-based extract or evanescent flavoring) and any kind of anticrystallization agent (pretty much always cream of tartar, but lemon juice works in a pinch, too) at the end. Done!

Caramel sauce is the inverse: you start with just sugar, water, and some sort of syrup (more on that in a few), maybe some sea salt, and bring that to a thrillingly high temperature, then add your fat (coconut milk and coconut oil, typically) and flavoring agents.

Caramel sauce is more syrupy (saucy, you could even say), so it's more forgiving and loose than its candy cousin. You want to emphasize the deep flavor of the toasty sugar—the fat is just for body and mouthfeel. Caramel candies need that fat to build structure, and are about more than just the flavor of sugar. They have chew and heft, so adding the fatty ingredients from the beginning helps create a good texture.

It's a good idea to check out "About the Recipes" on page 14 for notes about pot size and recipe measurements before jumping into these.

These recipes have a lot of salt by volume because we use a very fluffy, light fleur de sel salt that weighs about half that of regular table salt. Fleur de sel sea salt is any kind of flaky, large-grained sea salt that you like. If a recipe calls for fleur de sel sea salt but you only have table salt, that's just fine—just use the same **weight** if you're measuring in grams, but halve the **measurement**; that is, if a recipe calls for 2 tablespoons/16 g of fleur de sel sea salt, use 1 tablespoon **or** 16 g of regular salt.

ON CRYSTALLIZATION; OR, LEARNING TO LOVE SYRUP AND HATE STIRRING

Depending on your perspective, nothing really ruins caramel. Really black-burnt caramel is probably garbage, but short of that, you can always make something usable. Crystallized caramel is usually fixable, and burnt caramel is often better than caramel that's not overcooked. If you're flexible with your expectations of a recipe, you'll always make something great.

That said, the two most common causes of "ruined" caramel are crystallization and burning.

Most caramel candies and sauces, except for the most thin and quickly used, include some sort of syrup, also called invert sugar. I know you'll be tempted not to use the syrup mentioned in these recipes. Sugar's sugar, right? Why go buy another form of it, just use more sugar! Sure. It might be fine! But syrup (in collaboration with a few other tricks we'll get to) is your insurance policy against crystalized confections. Crystallized caramel is crumbly, crunchy, cloudy, and not pourable—you'll know it when you see it. It's fixable and it's not the end of the world, but let's just use syrup and good technique and not have to deal with it, okay?

Also: syrup is so great! Please let me hype you up about the badassery and general radness of syrup in candy making here.

Syrup teaches your caramel how to behave like a civilized human being. It "seeds" the caramel and hand-holds its molecules in the right direction, away from crystallization, toward lush unspoiled velvety sugary purity. Syrup ensures your confections have a smooth and perfect mouthfeel, and in frozen desserts, such as sorbet, gelato, and ice cream, it helps reduce iciness and keeps a soft and smooth texture. Replacing part of the sugar with syrup in baked goods makes them more tender and moist. Syrup makes your confections have a longer shelf life, helps control bacteria, carries flavors and aromas efficiently (resulting in a tastier recipe), and contributes to beautiful caramelized flavor. Syrup!

You can use any old syrup, really—you just need a liquid form of sugar that isn't crystallized.

Most commercial invert sugars aren't technically vegan, though, because they're made with refined white cane sugar, which typically uses bone char from cow bones as a filtering agent. Beet sugar, organic sugar, and raw sugars are always vegan, so any syrups made with these is vegan.

Industrial candy makers and most "artisan" confectioners use industrially made invert syrup, glucose syrup (a highly refined sugar syrup) and/or corn syrup (high fructose or not, as suits the product), which is superrefined and typically genetically modified.

For a while, we used organic corn syrup as our invert sugar because it's not genetically modified and works perfectly. But it's insanely expensive and we got tired of listing corn in all our ingredients. Finally, we started making our own cane syrup. We immediately felt like idiots for ever using corn syrup. Homemade cane syrup is ridiculously easy, is the perfect intro recipe for newbie shop workers just starting their caramel life, keeps forever, and is a million times cheaper than any ready-made store-bought syrup. It's useful in most of the recipes in this book. Thinned out, it makes a simple syrup-type sweetener for coffee or iced tea, meaning lemonade or sangria or homemade soda syrups for flavored seltzers are five minutes away at all times—once you have it in the house you'll find uses for it every day.

But if you don't want to make a recipe before you make your recipe, even one you can make in a big batch and have ready at all times (do it!), you can buy syrup. Organic corn syrup is best, or, in descending order of efficacy/loveliness, you can use glucose syrup, British golden syrup, brown rice syrup, agave syrup, maple syrup, barley malt syrup, or light molasses. You can also buy a thing called Trimoline, which is a processed magical nonvegan (bones!) uncrystalizable invert sugar that I've never used.

The other secret ingredient to make caramel that isn't as prone to crystallizing is cream of tartar. Yes, cream of tartar is vegan. It's a by-product of winemaking, an acid that helps prevent sugar crystals from forming. If you don't have cream of tartar and want to make your caramel recipe anyway, just use twice as much lemon juice or vinegar (lemon is better) as cream of tartar called for.

cane syrup
....

Cane syrup is our #1 kitchen workhorse, the base for all of our caramel candies. It's also dead easy and a perfect first caramel preparation. At our shop, we make it using 25 pounds of sugar at a time, twice a week or so. Here's a slightly smaller version. This recipe scales up perfectly, and keeps for two months at cool room temperature.

Makes 2 cups syrup

1 cup/240 g water
2¾ cups/570 g sugar
¾ teaspoon/3 g cream of tartar
⅛ teaspoon/pinch of sea salt

1. Combine all the ingredients in a 2- to 4-quart pot and gently stir together, being careful not to splash too much on the sides of the pan.
2. Bring to a slow boil and cook over medium-low heat—the mixture should be healthily bubbling but not climbing the sides of the pot.
3. Brush the sides of the pot with a pastry brush dipped in water once in a while, to prevent crystallization.
4. Cook until the syrup comes to 237°F. The temperature of this syrup isn't too important. If it only gets to 235°F or so, your syrup will just be a little more watery, but that's okay. Try not to let it get above 238°F, only because then it gets a little too thick to work with easily.
5. Turn off the heat and let the syrup cool in the pot. Pour the room-temperature syrup into a container and store, tightly covered, at room temperature or in the refrigerator. Refrigerated syrup will be more difficult to use, so let it sit at room temperature for a few hours before using, if you can.

STIRRING

Syrup and cream of tartar are good insurance policies against any untoward textural issues with your caramel, but they aren't magic. Technique is a form of magic, however. Technique, when it comes to caramel, basically boils down (it's a pun!) to: don't stir.

The primary difference between regular cooking and caramel making is stirring. You can stir your tomato sauce as much as you want and it'll be fine, but if you stir caramel too much, it could crystallize because (I swear I'm not making this up) stirring splashes caramel-to-be onto the sides of the pot, which could dry out, get funky (out of ideal sugar-molecule alignment),

drop back into the pot, and convince all the other sugar molecules to misbehave as well. Caramel is extremely prone to bullying and peer pressure.

To prevent crystallization, just stir as little as possible—when you put all your ingredients in the pot, it's fine to stir to mix them, but then hold off unless you're worried about burning. Once in a while, you'll want to poke around in the pot with a spatula, and when your caramel comes up to temperature and you need to fold in your final flavorings (ephemeral ingredients, such as vanilla beans, which lose their flavor with long cooking), you'll need to whisk them in thoroughly, but avoid jauntily stirring or whisking in a way that causes a lot of splashes.

You can also dip a pastry brush (make sure it's a high-heat stable one, such as a silicone brush) into a jar of water and run it around the edge of your caramel in the pot a few times, to neutralize any crystalized rascals that might be hanging around. (Don't do this obsessively every minute as new chocolatiers always want to do in our shop, or you'll add a lot of water to the pot, which could throw off your recipe.) Or you can just keep the lid on your pot, and condensation will do the work of a wet pastry brush. I like this method the best. I have no patience for this pastry brush business, but the recipes in this book use the pastry brush method because it's a little more user-friendly, since the open pot allows you to monitor your caramel. If you go the lidded route, know that your caramel might cook a little faster than the recipe says because of the increased heat from the closed lid.

If you do your best and the universe wasn't aligned to make caramel that day and your recipe comes out crystalized anyway, don't worry; it's usually fixable. To fix crystalized caramel, add a tablespoon or two of water to your recipe and ¼ teaspoon of cream of tartar or lemon juice, then (in a clean pot), cook the caramel to 1 or 2 degrees higher than the recipe states. In most cases this will bring you back to caramel perfection. If it doesn't, remember that crystallization only affects texture, not flavor—just enjoy your creation anyway. Or add a little coconut milk or water and melt it down to make a sauce.

The Hazelnut Praline recipe in this book uses intentionally crystallized caramel, proving that taste really is all a matter of perspective. If you're curious about the ins and outs of crystallization, make it to get a feel for what not to do with every other recipe in this book—basically, stir like crazy.

ON BURNT CARAMEL

Burnt caramel is such a desired flavor that it's sold as an extract, used as a marketing term, induces visions of loveliness in all who, like my mother did, crave burnt flavors. Burnt caramel has a bitter note that I love. Most of the time, if you overcook your caramel a few degrees you'll just have a deeper, richer caramel. If you're making caramel candies, you might have candies that are harder than you wanted, more of a suckable confection than a chewable one. You can refer to them as burnt toffees instead of caramels and call it a day, or, if you like the flavor but not the texture, you can add a tablespoon or two of water and a little lemon juice and gently remelt your recipe, then form as directed, or make into a sauce—see the index for recipes.

If you suspect your caramel is burning, investigate with a spatula, but don't attempt to scrape up the bottom of the pan to stop the burning or you'll incorporate potentially bitter burnt bits into your recipe. Pour the caramel into a clean pot, soak the burnt pot in the sink, and continue with your recipe.

If you like the flavor of your creation, you've made a successful confection, even if it wasn't the texture you're looking for. Be malleable, and you'll always make something great.

CARAMEL SAUCES AND SYRUPS

Caramel sauces and syrups don't need the structure of caramel candies, so they cook quicker and have simpler ingredient lists. They're a good way to limber up your caramel-making muscles.

Basic Caramel Sauce (page 104)

melon with shichimi togarashi syrup

··

I love Pete Taliaferro's heirloom melons and buy way too many of them in late summer from the farm two blocks from my house. This recipe is for gorgeous fresh summertime melons whose flavor you want to slightly amplify without masking their essential perfection. A spicy syrup balances the ridiculous sweetness of a good ripe melon, and turns a summertime fruit plate into something complex and sophisticated. When we were testing this out at the shop, everyone went nuts for it. I brought the tester batches to our café and they made their way into lattes that gained a cult following. I like our customers.

Shichimi togarashi is a Japanese seven-spice powder. You can buy it in most Asian markets and some supermarkets, or you can make it yourself, which (surprise!) is what I like to do. A recipe follows. If your shichimi is coarse, grind it a little in a spice grinder.

Makes 2 cups syrup

2½ cups/500 g sugar

1 cup plus 2 tablespoons/250 g water

2 tablespoons/16 g finely ground shichimi togarashi

Ripe seasonal melon: cantaloupe, watermelon, muskmelon, etc., thinly sliced

Mint, edible flowers, or other garnishes as desired

Sea salt

1. Combine the sugar and water in a 2- to 4-quart pot and bring to a slow boil, stirring once or twice but otherwise leaving alone. When the syrup comes to a boil, add the shichimi togarashi and cook over medium heat until thick and syrupy and two shades darker, about 30 minutes. Lower the heat if the syrup starts climbing the sides of the pan.
2. If possible, let the syrup sit overnight at room temperature, covered in the pot or in a covered container, then strain. Or strain after letting the syrup sit for an hour or as much time as you have.

3.   Slice the melon thinly and arrange nicely on a plate or platter. Drizzle the syrup over the melon and garnish with herbs, flowers, or anything that looks beautiful and edible in your garden, farmers' market, or windowsill at the moment. Nasturtiums, with their peppery bite and fiery colors, are a particularly nice match, and they're supereasy to grow, too. Sprinkle a little salt over everything.

Homemade Shichimi Togarashi

This makes a lot! But once you have it, you'll want it around. It keeps for months in the refrigerator or a dark part of your kitchen cabinets. Sprinkle it on anything that needs a little extra salty nutty fruity lightly spicy nice flavor.

Makes about 1½ cups shichimi togarashi

2 tablespoons/30 g freshly ground black pepper

½ cup/15 g dried tangerine peel (let some tangerine peels hang out until they get nicely dried up, or dry in a low oven)

¼ cup/35 g ground red chile pepper (we use single-chile powders, such as ancho or chipotle, but if you want to use chili powder, go for it)

2 tablespoons/15 g ground nori or other seaweed

¼ cup/40 g black sesame seeds

¼ cup/45 g white poppy seeds or nigella seeds

2 tablespoons/20 g garlic powder

1.   Combine all the ingredients in a bowl. If your mixture seems too coarse, grind it a little in a spice grinder or food processor or mortar and pestle. If it seems too moist, let it dry out at room temperature for a few days or in a low oven for an hour or so.

basic caramel sauce

Caramel sauce is made differently from caramel candies, and this is confusing. Really, you can make either one either way, but it's slightly better to make them their own specific ways, so let's do it. Sometimes "slightly better" is really the best.

Caramel candies need most of their ingredients to be cooked together to form a nice cohesive, chewy structure that will hold up on its own. Caramel sauce is quicker and easier: just burn sugar, add some fat for texture, and you're done. (You're free to also thin out a failed caramel candy recipe with water and use it as caramel sauce.)

Try to never refrigerate caramel sauces made with coconut oil, or the oil might separate out and harden. If this happens, just warm and stir to reincorporate the oil.

Makes 2 cups sauce

2 cups/400 g sugar

2 scant tablespoons/30 g Cane Syrup (page 96) or organic corn syrup

¼ cup/56 g water

1 teaspoon/5 g cream of tartar

½ teaspoon/3 g sea salt

½ cup/120 g coconut milk

1 teaspoon/5 g pure vanilla extract

1. Combine the sugar, syrup, water, cream of tartar, and salt in a 2-quart pot and bring to a boil over medium heat. Cook until the syrup is a very dark amber color and registers 300°F on a candy thermometer.
2. Remove from the heat and add the milk very carefully—the caramel will bubble up and spit. Stir with a rubber spatula or whisk. Stir thoroughly to ensure it is very well emulsified.
3. Let cool for a few minutes, then stir in the vanilla.
4. Let cool at room temperature for an hour or so, then pour into squeeze bottles or a container.
5. Do not refrigerate if planning on using this sauce within 3 weeks or so. For longer storage, refrigerate, then warm and stir to incorporate any oils before using.

(recipe photo shown on page 99)

piloncillo chile caramel sauce

· ·

Piloncillo is a toasty, minimally refined brown sugar that comes in a cone or block. Regular light or dark brown sugar will work in this recipe, but piloncillo has a nice smoked, dirty flavor that makes a superior caramel sauce. Light brown sugar will cook a little faster and dark brown sugar will be a little more prone to burning, but will make a lush, deeply browned caramel; however, neither one will give you the exact flavor of piloncillo.

Because the dark sugars can obscure the caramelization process, force yourself to cook this one a bit longer than you feel comfortable with, otherwise it will end up too thin.

One of our chocolatiers, Sam, tested this recipe out and reported that I'd unintentionally re-created the flavors of a childhood sweet of hers, Pulparindo, a sweet-spicy tamarind candy.

This sauce is truly and vibrantly spicy. Use less spice if you want a less spicy sauce, or no spice. Or more spice. Go nuts, you.

Makes 1¾ cups sauce

2 packed cups/400 g piloncillo sugar

2 tablespoons/42 g Cane Syrup (page 96) or organic corn syrup

1½ cups/360 g coconut milk

½ teaspoon/3 g freshly squeezed lemon juice

½ teaspoon/3 g sea salt

1 tablespoon/10 g ancho chile powder

1 teaspoon/3 g chipotle chile powder

1 tablespoon/15 g pure vanilla extract

1. Combine the sugar, syrup, 1 cup/240 g of the milk, and the lemon juice, salt, ancho powder, and chipotle powder in a 2-quart pot and bring to a boil over medium heat. Cook until the syrup is a dark golden amber color and registers 280°F on a candy thermometer.
2. Remove from the heat and carefully add the remaining ½ cup/120 g of milk. Stir with a rubber spatula or whisk.
3. Let cool for a few minutes, then stir in the vanilla.
4. Let cool at room temperature for an hour or so, then pour into squeeze bottles or glass jars.
5. Do not refrigerate if planning on using this sauce within 3 weeks or so. For longer storage, refrigerate, then warm and stir to incorporate oil before using.

maple caramel sauce

· ···

If you want a caramel sauce that's entirely refined sugar-free and, if you're on the East Coast, probably locally sourced, here you go. Don't try to pretend it's healthy, though. But it tastes so good, autumnal to the max and all that.

Makes ¾ cup sauce

1¼ cups/400 g dark pure maple syrup

¼ cup/60 g plus ⅓ cup/94 g coconut milk

½ teaspoon/3 g freshly squeezed lemon juice

½ teaspoon/3 g sea salt

1 teaspoon/5 g pure vanilla extract

1. Combine the maple syrup, ¼ cup/60 g of the milk, and the lemon juice and salt in a 2-quart pot and bring to a boil over medium heat. Cook until the syrup is a dark golden amber color and registers 270°F on a candy thermometer.
2. Remove from the heat and carefully add the ⅓ cup/94 g of milk. Stir with a rubber spatula or whisk.
3. Let cool for a few minutes, then stir in the vanilla.
4. Let cool at room temperature for an hour or so, then pour into squeeze bottles or glass jars.
5. Do not refrigerate if planning on using this sauce within 3 weeks or so. For longer storage, refrigerate, then warm and stir to incorporate any oils before using.

miso caramel sauce

· ·

MISO. Miso in desserts has become a done thing and, unlike pretty much all other food trends from the dawn of time, it's almost never a bad idea. Adding a bit of fermenty, salty depth to caramel balances sweetness with a rich complexity that makes everything you make more interesting.

I like white (shiro) miso in desserts—it's a sweet, young miso that complements sugar nicely. But truly any miso works. If you for some reason don't want soy, use a chickpea or barley miso. If you want a saltier, wilder caramel sauce, use a longer-aged miso, such as a red miso.

If you love miso in desserts, see White Miso and Black Sesame Caramels (page 164) and White Miso Truffles (page 67), and go to page 108 for an even more savory miso caramel sauce.

This is the basic caramel sauce of my heart, what I want on ice cream, cookie sandwiches, licked off my fingers in sex ways, yadda yadda.

Makes 1¾ cups sauce

3 tablespoons/40 g white or red miso

1¼ cups/300 g coconut milk

2 cups/400 g sugar

2 tablespoons/40 g Cane Syrup (page 96) or organic corn syrup

1. Whisk together the miso and 1 cup/240 g of the milk in a small bowl until smooth.
2. Combine the sugar, syrup, and miso mixture in a 2-quart pot and bring to a boil over medium heat. Cook until the syrup is a dark golden amber color and registers 270°F on a candy thermometer. Scrape the bottom of the pot occasionally with a spatula to prevent the miso from burning.
3. Remove from the heat and add the remaining ¼ cup/60 g of milk carefully. Stir with a rubber spatula or whisk.
4. Let cool at room temperature for an hour or so, then strain into squeeze bottles or glass jars.
5. Do not refrigerate if planning on using this sauce within 3 weeks or so. For longer storage, refrigerate, then warm and stir to incorporate any oils before using.

miso vinegar butterscotch

· ·

When I first started making candy, I was a deprived vegan just happy to have some candy in my life that fulfilled childhood cravings. Then, I wanted a little bit of salt in everything to take the edge off the cloying sweetness. Now, I'm grown up and pay property taxes and vote in school board elections, and I want not only salt but also tart flavors in everything, to introduce even more complexity and because simplistic sweet desserts are boring as hell. This is my current caramel sauce 3.0: sweet, mega-salty, just vinegary enough.

This recipe is a heavily modified rip-off from Momofuku's Miso Butterscotch, the same premise but mostly different ingredients and a different technique: Christina Tosi toasts miso and butter in the oven to brown the milk solids and burn the miso. I get a similar result by cooking everything slowly in a pot, like traditional caramel, and the finished sauce is glossier and saucier and veganier.

This sauce is tart and very salty. I like it that way, but you can use less vinegar and miso to calm it down a little if you want (or, in the parlance of our chocolate shop, "clam down." Why do kitchens, in particular, have these strange languages of their own? To mark difference from the world that doesn't stand up for fifteen hours a day?). I use apple cider vinegar because it's not too sour and has a good fruitiness, but sherry (what the Momofuku crew uses) is lovely, too. Bonus hot tip: balsamic miso butterscotch is something totally different, supremely weird, darkly rad.

Instead of regular coconut milk, this sauce uses sweetened condensed coconut milk, which is available in most health food stores and supermarkets. It's a nice shortcut to true butterscotch flavor, because it's already sweet and caramelly. If you can't find it, use regular full-fat coconut milk and a tablespoon more brown sugar.

Makes 2 cups butterscotch

3 tablespoons/50 g white miso

1 cup/240 g sweetened condensed coconut milk

1 cup/250 g water

6 tablespoons/60 g apple cider vinegar

2 cups/400 g light brown sugar

2 tablespoons/42 g Cane Syrup (page 96) or organic corn syrup

1 teaspoon/6 g sea salt

1. With a small wire whisk, whisk together the miso and milk in a small bowl until smooth.
2. Combine 3 tablespoons (30 g) of the water and 2 tablespoons (20 g) of the vinegar in a separate small bowl. Set aside.
3. Combine the miso mixture with the brown sugar, cane syrup, and salt in a 2- to 4-quart pot and bring to a boil over medium-low heat. Cook until the syrup is a dark golden amber color and registers 248°F on a candy thermometer.
4. Remove from the heat and let cool for a few minutes. Add the remaining 2 tablespoons/20 g of vinegar and 3 tablespoons/30 g of water.
5. Let cool at room temperature for an hour or so, then strain into squeeze bottles or glass jars.
6. Do not refrigerate if planning on using this sauce within 3 weeks or so. For longer storage, refrigerate, then warm and stir to incorporate any oils before using.

caramel apples

Every year for Halloween I dress as someone + John Waters. I'd been searching for a way to publicly and periodically acknowledge my affection for John Waters, and in Halloween I found it. Acid-washed jeans, suspenders, and an orange vest with a thin swipe of eyeliner above my top lip = Marty McFly John Waters. Mary Tyler Moore with a mustache and sensible corduroy belted jumpsuit. A drop-waist linen dress and cloche with delicate but florid mustache for a Virginia Woolf John Waters. Scout Finch as a ham as John Waters, a faint but visible black line above her lip peeking out from a very nonvegan ham costume. I wasn't into dressing up as a kid, but New Paltz is a Halloween town, so why not.

And all season long, we make these caramel apples. It's been a whole ordeal. But we've cracked it, and you don't have to go through it. And they taste way better than you think they will. So:

Typically, confectioners buy butterscotch caramel (basically melted supermarket wrapped caramels) by the bucket, barely warm it, and dip apples in it. Lacking such luxuries and also realizing we'd have nothing to complain about if we had shortcuts like that, we Laverne & Shirley'd it and did it our way.

Superstitiously, we still take some precautions. Dip your apples all the way up to their necks, right up to the stick, so the caramel has some strong shoulders to grip onto. We also dip the finished caramel apples into a superthin coating of dark chocolate (we thin ours with a little melted cocoa butter to make a nice crispy shell), which is optional. The wet chocolate is a nice canvas for such toppings as toasted nuts, fancy sea salt, more chopped chocolate, chopped dried fruit, cookie or graham cracker crumbs—go for it.

Eat your apples right away, or store in an airtight container in the refrigerator for several weeks.

Makes 4 to 6 caramel apples

8 medium-size or small tart apples

1 cup/240 g coconut milk

1¼ cups/297 g packed brown sugar

¼ cup/69 g Cane Syrup (page 96) or organic corn syrup

½ teaspoon/3 g pure vanilla extract

½ teaspoon cream of tartar

1 pound chocolate, for dipping

Toppings of choice

Special equipment: caramel apple sticks

1. Hammer the sticks into the apples. Line a sheet pan with parchment paper.
2. Combine the milk, brown sugar, and syrup in a 2- to 4-quart pot over medium heat. Heat to 259°F.
3. Remove from the heat. Whisk in the vanilla and cream of tartar.
4. Immediately pour the caramel into a tall container that will fit an apple when dipped into it (we use a tall 4-cup measuring cup).
5. Dip the apples into the caramel all the way to the stick and place on the prepared sheet pan. Let cool for 30 minutes, or until completely set up.
6. When the apples are cool, temper the chocolate (see page 17) and dip the apples into it, then roll the apples in your preferred toppings or sprinkle the toppings on the apples while the chocolate is wet.

CARAMEL CANDIES

One step past caramel sauce is caramel candy.

Caramel candies are so cool. They tread the line between solid and liquid: when cool, the former; when warm, the latter. They're everything at once encased in a thin skin, just trying to keep their insides in—like you, like me.

The only trick with caramel candy is to pay attention to what it wants in terms of temperature. Cook it to the right temperature, pour it hot, dip it cold, eat it at room temperature. I want you to feel the great sense of accomplishment that comes from realizing how easy it truly is to get your sugar molecules to behave like they should.

One paradox of caramel is that you want to cook it fairly quickly, so, strangely, it doesn't get too caramelized. You want to taste the flavorings you're putting into your caramel, not just burnt sugar, so cook it on as high heat as you can without it climbing the pan and boiling over so your additions shine through the plain caramel flavor.

Kindly review "On Crystallization" (see page 94) before starting your first caramel candy recipe, so you know why you're doing what you're doing in these recipes.

If you're working your way through this book sequentially (yes!) and are now a pro at dipping truffles in tempered chocolate, caramel is exactly the same except that caramels are generally square and truffles are generally round. Instead of using a truffle dipper, you might want to splurge on something called a dipping fork ($2 or so, generally) that will help lift caramels into and out of chocolate handily. Or a regular fork works just fine, as do your own two hands, which make nice thin chocolate coatings that look charmingly rustic.

There are two ways to flavor caramel. Once you understand the difference, you can concoct your own flavor combinations with abandon.

INFUSIONS are sturdy, long-cooking flavorings that are added at the beginning or middle of the cooking process. More substantial ingredients that need to be incorporated fully into the caramel are added during the cooking process (typically not at the beginning, because they could burn), so they cook with the caramel. Most spices, nut butters, vinegars, fruit and vegetable purees, and some alcohols are added while cooking.

ADDITIONS are ephemeral ingredients that can't stand up to the rigors of hot sugar and are added when cooking is finished. Tender herbs, extracts, most alcohols, and some spices are added at the end of cooking so they don't burn and/or so their gentle flavor isn't lost.

Caramel candies stay at perfect freshness for two months or more at cool room temperature or stored in an airtight container in the refrigerator. Be sure to let them come to room temperature before eating.

Master Method for Caramel Candy
Super important! Read and refer back to while making caramel candies!

Every caramel candy recipe has pretty much the same procedure, so here's more in-depth information about it. **If your specific recipe contradicts these instructions, go with what your recipe says.**

1. Set up your *mise en place* just like a line cook: get everything for the recipe ready ahead of time because once the recipe starts cooking, you won't have time to be measuring ingredients. Dump most of your ingredients into a pot. Almost all these recipes use a 2- to 4-quart pot. Use a good heavy-bottomed one. Turn the heat on at sort of a medium-low kind of thing. Stir a little to combine, then try not to stir.

2. Cook your caramel at a brisk bubble: it shouldn't be climbing the sides of the pot, but it shouldn't be standing still. Cook it as high as you can without its starting to climb.

3. While the mixture is cooking, wash down the sides of the pan with a pastry brush dipped in cool water every 10 minutes or so, to prevent sugar crystals from forming on the side of the pot, jumping into the caramel, and making it gritty.

4. If your caramel bubbles up rapidly and almost boils over (or boils over), turn it out into a clean pot and continue to cook rather than attempting to wash off all the caramel on the side of the pot with a wet pastry brush, which will add a lot of water to your recipe.

5. Take the temperature of the caramel once in a while. Don't rest the thermometer probe on the bottom or sides of the pot; keep it about midway into the caramel in the center of the pot. When it gets within 5° to 10°F of the finished temperature, hang out with it while watching the temperature.

This is a great time to chill out and practice mindfulness. At this point, do not leave the caramel alone. An unattended caramel within 5°F or so of its finished temperature could burn in a minute, and once it comes up to temperature, it needs to be poured into molds immediately, before it sets up. The next few steps are quick.

6. When the caramel hits the desired temperature, don't freak. Keep the thermometer in long enough to ensure it really is at that temperature, and didn't randomly zoom up for a second.

7. Immediately stir in any additional ingredients the recipe calls for. Worry more that they are evenly incorporated into the caramel than about the stirring thing, since your caramel is done cooking.

8. Immediately and carefully pour caramel into molds or prepared pan (see next section). Let set up for 20 minutes, or until slightly firm, then cover with plastic wrap and freeze.

9. Let cool, cut into squares or pop out of the molds, and either wrap in confectionery paper or waxed paper or dip in melted chocolate.

Important Information About Forming Caramel Candies

Investing in a silicone caramel mold or two will make your candy-making life so much easier. Kitchenware supply stores and the Internet will have lots of options. We use 1 by 1-inch Chocoflex brand molds. Each has fifty-four cavities and will work for one recipe. Freezing your filled caramel mold before dipping it into chocolate will ensure your caramels keep their shape while dipping them.

If you want to cut your caramels by hand instead of pouring them into a mold, you can, but I'm not going to pretend that it's not harder. Here's how: completely line a 6-inch square silicone pan or small sheet pan with parchment paper. Be sure the parchment lines the sides of the pan. Wet the underside of the parchment before fitting it to the pan if it's being curly and uncooperative.

When the caramel is finished, pour it into the prepared pan and let set up for 20 minutes, or until slightly firm, then cover with plastic wrap and refrigerate until you're ready to cut your caramels. Don't freeze your caramels, as directed in the recipe, if you're going to cut them by hand.

Turn out onto another parchment-lined sheet pan (don't worry about lining the sides), then use a serrated or chef's knife—dipped frequently into hot water (a tall, conical container is best to hold it, such as a 4-cup liquid measuring cup or flower vase) and dried with a clean kitchen towel—to cut the square into 1-inch rows and then each row into 1-inch pieces, for three dozen

pieces (the thickness of your piece will depend on the caramel recipe you're making). Some recipes might require two pans.

CARAMEL CANDIES DIPPED IN CHOCOLATE

Here are recipes for a caramel that is dipped in tempered chocolate and garnished with sea salt or other flavorings. A thin chocolate coating ensures your caramel doesn't melt into a puddle before it makes its way to your mouth and adds another layer of texture and flavor, but if you don't want to mess with it you can cook your caramel to 1°F higher than indicated in the recipe, and wrap the cut caramels into waxed confectionery paper, which you can get in kitchen supply stores or online (sometimes labeled as "confectionery twisting paper"). Regular waxed paper works just fine, too; you'll just need to cut it to size. Cooking the caramel to a just slightly higher temperature ensures your caramel keeps its shape when its paper is unwrapped.

vanilla caramel master recipe

· ·

You can use this recipe as a template to make your own flavors, or make it to get the gist of how making caramel candies works before jumping into the flavor variations that follow, all of which build on this basic formula. If you use this recipe as a jumping-off point for other flavorings, reduce the amount of vanilla by half.

This recipe makes a lot. Sometimes smaller recipes crystallize more quickly, and since caramel candies keep for at least two months, I haven't made it smaller.

Makes 54 caramels

1 cup/240 g coconut milk

¼ cup/42 g coconut oil

1¾ cups/375 g sugar

½ cup/139 g Cane Syrup (page 96) or organic corn syrup

2 teaspoons/6 g fleur de sel sea salt

3 vanilla beans, split and scraped

2 teaspoons/7 g pure vanilla extract

1 teaspoon/6 g cream of tartar

1 pound chocolate, for dipping

Garnish: flaky sea salt

1. Combine the milk, oil, sugar, syrup, and salt in a 2- to 4-quart pot. Stir gently, then bring to a boil over medium heat without stirring. While the mixture is cooking, wash down the sides of the pan with a pastry brush dipped in cool water every 10 minutes or so, to prevent sugar crystals from forming on the side of the pot, jumping into the caramel, and making it gritty.

2. Cook over medium-low heat (the mixture should be simmering, but not climbing the sides of the pan) until the caramel registers 260°F on a candy thermometer.

3. Turn off the heat and stir in vanilla bean scrapings, vanilla, and cream of tartar with a whisk.
4. Carefully pour the caramel into molds or a prepared pan (see page 114). Let set up for 20 minutes, or until slightly firm, then cover with plastic wrap and freeze.
5. Keep the caramels in the freezer in their molds or pan so they keep their shape. Temper the chocolate (see page 17) and dip the caramels into it, using a dipping fork, regular fork, or your fingers. Garnish with flaky salt while the chocolate is wet.

apple cider and apple cider vinegar caramels with apple

· ·

We make a lot of apple confections because we live in apple country. This one is my favorite. Triple apple. One time our chocolatier Lucy was making Apple Caramels and the thermometer broke. No one could find the other one (I've since bought a stash of ten so this never happens again). She got very quiet and we watched her take the pot off the stove at a seemingly random moment. A degree or two difference in caramel temperatures, in a commercial operation, is the difference between salable confections and not. We kept asking her how she knew. "I listened to it," she said.

I can see why Lucy has a special bond with these. They're especially soft, not in texture but in flavor. An introverted, poetic caramel, like Lucy, whose heart beats pure poetry like no one I've ever met. The softies are always the best.

This caramel cooks to a much higher temperature than one without a fruit puree, because the fruit makes the mixture softer so the sugar needs to be cooked to a higher degree to set up properly. If you start to suspect that the mixture is burning, gently investigate with a wooden or silicone spoon. If the mixture is a bit burnt on the bottom but is close to the proper temperature, don't stress, just don't stir the pot (literally and also figuratively). When you pour the caramel out when it reaches the correct temperature, leave the burnt part in the pan, if possible. If it's looking burnt in a worrying way, transfer into a clean pot (don't scrape the sides or bottom of the pan, just pour the mixture in and put the burnt pan in the sink) and continue to cook.

Makes 42 caramels

½ cup/120 g coconut milk

3 tablespoons/38 g apple cider

3 tablespoons/28 g coconut oil

1 cup plus 3 tablespoons/240 g sugar

¼ cup/75 g Cane Syrup (page 96) or organic corn syrup

1 tablespoon/8 g fleur de sel sea salt

¼ cup/40 g apple cider vinegar

¼ cup/69 g applesauce, store-bought or homemade (recipe follows)

1 vanilla bean, split and scraped

1 teaspoon/4 g pure vanilla extract

1 teaspoon/5 g cream of tartar

1 pound chocolate, for dipping

Garnish: candied pecan pieces (see page 121)

1. Combine the milk, cider, oil, sugar, syrup, salt, and vinegar in a 2- to 4-quart pot. Stir gently, then bring to a boil over medium heat without stirring. While the mixture is cooking, wash down the sides of the pan with a pastry brush dipped in cool water every 5 minutes or so, to prevent sugar crystals from forming on the side of the pot, jumping into the caramel, and making it gritty.

2. Cook over medium-low heat (the mixture should be simmering, but not climbing the sides of the pan) until the caramel registers 250°F on a candy thermometer. Add the applesauce and cook until the caramel comes to 271°F.

3. Turn off the heat and stir in the vanilla bean scrapings, vanilla, and cream of tartar with a whisk.

4. Carefully pour the caramel into molds or a prepared pan (see page 114). Let set up for 20 minutes, or until slightly firm, then cover with plastic wrap and freeze.

5. Keep caramels in the freezer in their molds or pan so they keep their shape. Temper the chocolate (see page 17), and dip the caramels into it, using a dipping fork, regular fork, or your fingers. Garnish with candied pecans while the chocolate is wet.

Applesauce

We tend to use a tart apple, such as Pink Lady (my favorite, makes a nice pink applesauce whose color you'll never notice in the caramels), Idared, McIntosh, or Cortland, or an all-around good apple like Honeycrisp, Mutsu, or Fuji. A mix is even better than one variety.

1 apple (for Apple Caramels; but I encourage you to make more)

1. Peel your apples (if it's a Pink Lady or other pretty apple, save the peel, dry it out, and grind it in a spice grinder to garnish your apple creations), or, if you have a food mill, don't.
2. Chop the apples into big pieces and compost the cores. Cook your apples in a pot with nothing else over low heat, stirring often to make sure they don't burn, until they turn into applesauce. If you have a food mill, pass them through it and throw away the peels. Applesauce freezes beautifully.

Candied Nuts
for Apple Caramels and Life in General

This is a really great recipe! It's super easy and the nuts keep forever in a tightly sealed container in the fridge. Whip this one up for holidays, parties, package candied nuts in twee little bags with ribbon and a gift card for a good food gift, sprinkle these on a salad or roasted vegetables for extra-punchy crunchy flavor. Go wild.

We make this with pecans, using the broken nuts that are unfit to make Galapagos Turtle limbs (page 169) and use them to garnish Apple Caramels, but it works with most any nut. The pecans are flavored with fall spices that complement the autumnal Apple Caramels. We use the mixture of cinnamon, cloves, and nutmeg in this recipe for spicing local fresh-pressed apple cider as well.

Makes 2 cups nuts

¼ cup/55 g sugar

¾ teaspoon/5 g sea salt

1 recipe Apple Cider Spice (recipe follows) or other spice

2 tablespoons flaxseed egg whites (recipe follows)

2 cups/200 g pecans

1. Preheat the oven to 225°F. Line a half sheet pan (18 by 13 inches) with a silicone baking mat or parchment paper.
2. Combine the sugar, salt, and spice in a large bowl. In a separate bowl, whip the flaxseed egg whites for a minute with a fork or eggbeater. Add the nuts to the flaxseed egg whites, turning to coat. Add them to the spice mixture and toss to coat.
3. Spread evenly on the prepared sheet pans so the nuts aren't touching.
4. Bake for 15 minutes, then loosen and turn with a spatula. Continue to turn every 15 minutes until the nuts are crisp and dry, about 1 hour 15 minutes total.
5. Remove from the oven and let cool completely before packing into containers.

Here are some other flavor and nut combinations to try:

- **Five-Spice Cashews:** 1 tablespoon of Chinese five-spice powder, ½ teaspoon of ground cardamom.
- **Curried Cashews:** 1½ teaspoons of garam masala or mild curry powder, ½ teaspoon of ground turmeric.
- **Spicy Cocoa Pecans:** 2 tablespoons of unsweetened cocoa powder, 1 tablespoon of chile powder, 1 teaspoon of ground cinnamon.
- **Matcha Almonds:** 1 teaspoon of ground ginger, ½ teaspoon of wasabi powder, 2 tablespoons of matcha green tea powder.
- **Spiced Spicy Walnuts:** ½ teaspoon of chipotle powder, 2 teaspoons of ground cinnamon, ½ teaspoon of ground cloves, ½ teaspoon of ground cardamom.
- **Lavender-Cardamom Almonds:** 2 teaspoons of lavender buds, 2 teaspoons of ground cardamom.

Apple Cider Spice for Candied Pecans

1 tablespoon/8 g ground cinnamon
1 teaspoon/2 g ground cloves
¼ teaspoon/1 g ground nutmeg

1. Stir together all the ingredients in a small bowl.

Flaxseed Egg Whites

You'll need to make flaxseed egg whites to candy your nuts. It's dead easy. No flax? Chia works, too. With this recipe, you'll have more egg white-type material than you need, but it freezes perfectly in an ice cube tray or resealable plastic bag.

2 tablespoons/14 g flaxseeds
1 cup/240 g water

1. Combine the flaxseeds and water in a small saucepan, bring to a boil, and boil until thickened.
2. Remove from the heat, then strain, saving the thick liquid and throwing out the flaxseeds (or use them to make more "eggs"—second batches are only slightly less eggy).

Spicy Apple Cider Caramels

For a spicy apple cider caramel, modify the recipe as follows:

1 Add ½ teaspoon of chipotle powder and a pinch of cayenne pepper (for a super spicy caramel, use ¼ teaspoon of cayenne. For a less spicy caramel, use no cayenne) to caramels when you add applesauce.

cardamom caramels

Floral and lush, these used to be an occasional item in our shop, but we missed them too much when they weren't around, so we made them a regular. This is a nice, light, fresh-tasting caramel.

Makes 54 caramels

¾ cup/180 g coconut milk

¼ cup/42 g coconut oil

1½ cups/300 g sugar

½ cup/150 g Cane Syrup (page 96) or organic corn syrup

1 tablespoon/8 g fleur de sel sea salt

1 vanilla bean, split and scraped

1 teaspoon/3 g pure vanilla extract

1½ teaspoons/3 g ground cardamom pods

2 teaspoons/9 g cream of tartar

1 pound chocolate, for dipping

Garnish: ground cardamom

1. Combine the milk, oil, sugar, syrup, and salt in a 2- to 4-quart pot. Stir gently, then bring to a boil over medium heat without stirring. While the mixture is cooking, wash down the sides of the pan with a pastry brush dipped in cool water every 10 minutes or so, to prevent sugar crystals from forming on the side of the pot, jumping into the caramel, and making it gritty.
2. Cook over medium-low heat (the mixture should be simmering, but not climbing the sides of the pan) until the caramel registers 261°F on a candy thermometer.
3. Turn off the heat and stir in the vanilla bean scrapings, vanilla, cardamom, and cream of tartar with a whisk.
4. Carefully pour the caramel into molds or a prepared pan (see page 114). Let set up for 20 minutes, or until slightly firm, then cover with plastic wrap and freeze.
5. Keep the caramels in the freezer in their molds or pan so they keep their shape. Temper the chocolate (see page 17), and dip the caramels into it, using a dipping fork, regular fork, or your fingers. Garnish with ground cardamom while the chocolate is wet.

cinnamon espresso fireball caramels

Red hot! Just a simple delicious spicy caffeinated baby.

Cinnamon extract is available online and in some supermarkets, but you can also skip it and add another ½ teaspoon of ground cinnamon. Coffee extract is widely available. Be sure to use freshly ground coffee for a nice, vibrant flavor.

We use soft-stick Mexican cinnamon, called canela, for our cinnamon needs. You need to grind it in a spice grinder, but it's worth it for the complex, flowery flavor, not as harsh as typical cinnamon. If you can't find canela cinnamon, any type of cinnamon works.

Makes 60 caramels

1 cup/240 g coconut milk

¼ cup/42 g coconut oil

1½ cups packed/362 g brown sugar

1 tablespoon/5 g espresso powder

½ cup/150 g Cane Syrup (page 96) or organic corn syrup

1 tablespoon/8 g fleur de sel sea salt

2 teaspoons/10 g cream of tartar

1½ teaspoons/3 g ground cinnamon

1 tablespoon/9 g ancho chile powder

1½ teaspoons/4 g cayenne pepper

½ teaspoon/1 g coffee extract

½ teaspoon/1 g cinnamon extract

1 pound chocolate, for dipping

Garnish: cinnamon powder and/or 1 cup tempered chocolate, for piping (optional)

1. Combine the milk, oil, brown sugar, espresso powder, syrup, and salt in a 2- to 4-quart pot. Stir gently, then bring to a boil over medium heat without stirring. While the mixture is cooking, wash down the sides of the pan with a pastry brush dipped in cool water every 10 minutes or so, to prevent sugar crystals from forming on the side of the pot, jumping into the caramel, and making it gritty.
2. Cook over medium-low heat (the mixture should be simmering, but not climbing the sides of the pan) until the caramel registers 256°F on a candy thermometer.
3. Turn off the heat and stir in the cream of tartar, cinnamon, chile powder, cayenne, and cinnamon extract with a whisk.
4. Carefully pour the caramel into molds or a prepared pan (see page 114).
5. Let set up for 20 minutes, or until slightly firm, then cover with plastic wrap and freeze.
6. Keep the caramels in the freezer in their molds or pan so they keep their shape. Temper the chocolate (see page 17), and dip the caramels into it, using a dipping fork, regular fork, or your fingers. Garnish with a sprinkle of cinnamon and/or, if you'd like, piped lines of tempered chocolate.

jenn's roasted plum and sage caramels

. . . .

It's taken me ten years or so, but I've come to see the people I work with as puzzles to unlock: what are they good at, how can we bring it out of them? Now, I try as much as possible to identify people's strengths and see where in the business they can be put to use. I mostly do this by hands-off managing, by letting things run as much as they can by themselves and seeing where everyone naturally lands. I've done this with Jenn more than any other manager we've ever had—Alexis and Kate and I promoted her to manager and didn't really give her any direction whatsoever. Sort of ridiculous. But suddenly she was there, doing things we didn't know we needed, filling all kinds of cracks, lifting us up, letting us know what she wanted to improve around the chocolate shop. She tightened up our recipes, strengthened our systems, kept us on track with long-term goals we were too preoccupied to remember. She's basically just a constant joy. In addition to her wide-ranging, focused work ethic, Jenn has a sunniness and optimism balanced by a complete lack of Pollyanna pie-in-the-sky-ism that works for our Gothy, secretly misanthropic shop greatly.

As part of a project where everyone in our shop created a confection, Jenn created these babies. Garden sage for a nice herby bass note, plus a glut of local plums creates a chewy, textured caramel, with white balsamic vinegar for bonus tartness.

Makes 50 caramels

½ cup plus 2 tablespoons/148 g coconut milk

¼ cup/42 g coconut oil

1 cup plus 1 tablespoon/242 g sugar

¼ cup plus 1 tablespoon/108 g Cane Syrup (page 96) or organic corn syrup

2 teaspoons/6 g fleur de sel sea salt

¼ cup plus 2¼ tablespoons/100 g Roasted Plum Puree (recipe follows)

1 teaspoon/5 g cream of tartar

5 teaspoons/3 g ground dried sage

2 tablespoons/30 g white balsamic vinegar

1 pound chocolate, for dipping

Garnish: fleur de sel sea salt and dried sage

1. Combine the milk, oil, sugar, syrup, and salt in a 2- to 4-quart pot. Stir gently, then bring to a boil over medium heat without stirring. While the mixture is cooking, wash down the sides of the pan with a pastry brush dipped in cool water every 10 minutes or so, to prevent sugar crystals from forming on the side of the pot, jumping into the caramel, and making it gritty.
2. Cook over medium-low heat (the mixture should be simmering, but not climbing the sides of the pan) until the caramel registers 250°F on a candy thermometer. Then, carefully fold in the plum puree and lower the heat to low. Carefully scrape the bottom of the pan with a spatula every 10 minutes or so to ensure that no plum puree is burning on the bottom of the pot. Cook over low heat until the caramel registers 262°F on a candy thermometer.
3. Turn off the heat and stir in the cream of tartar, sage, and vinegar with a whisk.
4. Carefully pour the caramel into molds or a prepared pan (see page 114). Let set up for 20 minutes, or until slightly firm, then cover with plastic wrap and freeze.
5. Keep the caramels in the freezer in their molds or pan so they keep their shape. Temper the chocolate (see page 17), and dip the caramels into it, using a dipping fork, regular fork, or your fingers. Garnish with a sprinkle of sea salt and sage while the chocolate is wet.

Roasted Plum Puree

Makes 1 cup puree

3 plums
3 tablespoons/40 g olive oil

1. Preheat the oven to 400°F. Line a sheet pan with parchment paper.
2. Cut the plums into quarters and remove the pits.
3. Lay out, skin side down, on the prepared sheet pan.
4. Brush with olive oil and roast until the plums are golden brown, 15 to 30 minutes.
5. Remove from the oven, let the plums cool, then puree in a blender until completely smooth.

lucy and shana's spicy peanut sauce caramels

· ·

Both these gem humans started working at the chocolate shop at roughly the same time. Lucy's the poet, Shana's the gonzo hedonist. A good mix, they brought out interesting elements in each other. Lucy's all softness, leaking words and art borne from introspection and a wildly open heart. Lucy is in love with Rudi, her childhood sweetheart. Rudi and Lucy grew up in New Paltz and so are inherent eccentrics. In our casual town filled with college kids who wear pajamas to brunch, Rudi has worn a suit every day since he could dress himself. A few years ago, Lucy and Rudi produced Henry, a small human composed entirely of cashew cheese and other live cultures.

Shana's the queen of a genre of humans I've come to understand as unique to New Paltz and the Hudson Valley: Long Island freaks exiled from Long Island. We've taken in many of these: black sheep of their families, vegans, queer people, weirdos of all stripes who grew up on the island and who found, in us, a way of being different from the malls and bars. Shana is always psyched about something. She is a principled bon vivant. When we interviewed Shana, she had chipped nail polish, which is a pet peeve of mine in interviews, but halfway through the interview she put her hands flat on the table and said in the Long Island cigarette voice she was born with, "Listen. I love this place. I want to be here. I'll work my ass off. You'll see. Just hire me, okay? I'll work really, really hard." We did, and she did.

Shana is exuberantly obsessed with peanut butter, and this caramel was the result of a collaboration between her and Lucy. Like both of them, it's entirely itself, entirely strange, highly lovable, and you will get obsessed with it. It's Thai peanut sauce in caramel form: spicy and sour and strange. Lime oil is available in some supermarkets and online. It's not an extract nor an essential oil; it's a potent culinary oil pressed from lime zest.

This caramel makes a large amount, but halving it doesn't work like we wanted it to. Its many flavors need room to stretch out in the pan.

Makes 87 caramels

1 cup/240 g coconut milk

⅓ cup/80 g rice vinegar

¼ cup/56 g coconut oil

2¼ cups/450 g sugar

½ cup/216 g Cane Syrup (page 92) or organic corn syrup

Heaping ¼ teaspoon/2 g ground, toasted cumin seeds

2 scant tablespoons/14 g fleur de sel sea salt

⅓ cup/90 g all-natural smooth peanut butter

¼ teaspoon/1 g culinary-grade lime oil (see headnote)

¾ teaspoon/2 g cayenne powder

¾ teaspoon/2 g chipotle powder

½ teaspoon/1 g ancho chile powder or chili powder

½ teaspoon/.8 g ground ginger

2 teaspoons/9 g cream of tartar

1 pound chocolate, for dipping

Garnish: red pepper flakes and fleur de sel sea salt

1. Combine the milk, vinegar, oil, sugar, syrup, cumin seeds, and salt in a 2- to 4-quart pot. Stir gently, then bring to a boil over medium heat without stirring. While the mixture is cooking, wash down the sides of the pan with a pastry brush dipped in cool water every 10 minutes or so, to prevent sugar crystals from forming on the side of the pot, jumping into the caramel, and making it gritty.

2. Cook over medium-low heat (the mixture should be simmering, but not climbing the sides of the pan) until the caramel registers roughly 245°F on a candy thermometer. Stir in the peanut butter. Once in a while, gently stir the pot to integrate the peanut butter into the whole and prevent it from clumping or burning.

3. Continue to cook until the caramel registers 260°F on a candy thermometer.

4. Turn off the heat and stir in the lime oil, cayenne and chile powders, ginger, and cream of tartar with a whisk, making sure the peanut butter is completely emulsified.

5. Carefully pour the caramel into molds or a prepared pan (see page 114). Let set up for 20 minutes, or until slightly firm, then cover with plastic wrap and freeze.

6. Keep the caramels in the freezer in their molds or pan so they keep their shape. Temper the chocolate (see page 17), and dip the caramels into it, using a dipping fork, regular fork, or your fingers. Garnish with a mix of red pepper flakes and fleur de sel sea salt while the chocolate is wet.

maple pecan caramels

· ·

No huge amount of salt in this one, no tart element, none of the crutches to big flavor we typically lean on. It's just umami: dark, rich, deep, mysterious, autumnal flavor. We use organic Arizona pecans that are so deeply toasted they're just barely shy of uselessly burnt and lots of local grade A extra-dark maple syrup.

This caramel tends to want to burn. If you're gently stirring and your spoon comes back from the depths of the pot with suspicious tar on the bottom, pour the caramel into a different pot. Don't scrape the black bits back into the caramel. That said, this caramel should be almost burnt. By the time it comes up to temperature, you'll be worried it's gone too far. That's how it should be.

Makes 45 caramels

¾ cup/80 g pecans

1 cup/240 g coconut milk
¼ cup/42 g coconut oil
1 cup/314 g pure maple syrup, preferably grade A extra-dark
½ cup/191 g Cane Syrup (page 96) or organic corn syrup
1 tablespoon/8 g fleur de sel sea salt
2 teaspoons/10 g pure vanilla extract
1 teaspoon/5 g cream of tartar
1 pound chocolate, for dipping
Garnish: candied pecans (page 121) or regular toasted pecans

1. Make pecan butter: toast the pecans in a preheated 375°F oven for 5 to 8 minutes, or until darkly roasted and fragrant. Remove from the oven, let cool, then grind to a perfectly fine butter in a food processor.

2. Combine the milk, oil, maple syrup, cane syrup, and salt in a 2- to 4-quart pot. Stir gently, then bring to a boil over medium heat without stirring. While the mixture is cooking, wash down the

sides of the pan with a pastry brush dipped in cool water every 10 minutes or so, to prevent sugar crystals from forming on the side of the pot, jumping into the caramel, and making it gritty.

3. Cook over medium-low heat (the mixture should be simmering, but not climbing the sides of the pan) until the caramel registers 250°F on a candy thermometer. Stir in the pecan butter, being careful not to overly agitate the caramel.

4. Cook over medium-low heat (the mixture should be simmering, but not climbing the sides of the pan) until the caramel registers 259° to 260°F on a candy thermometer.

5. Turn off the heat and beat in the vanilla and cream of tartar with a whisk.

6. Carefully pour the caramel into molds or a prepared pan (see page 114). Let set up for 20 minutes, or until slightly firm, then cover with plastic wrap and freeze.

7. Keep the caramels in the freezer in their molds or pan so they keep their shape. Temper the chocolate (see page 17), and dip the caramels into it, using a dipping fork, regular fork, or your fingers. Garnish with crushed toasted pecans while the chocolate is wet.

pumpKin spice caramels

True pumpkin spice flavor from squash, not pumpkin, which always tastes more pumpkiny than pumpkin, and fresh-ground spices. You can use canned pumpkin and preground spices, but a little more time and energy will give you a caramel several magnitudes more tasty. I promise not to judge you, either way.

We used to get this amazing heirloom squash from a local farm, Wright's Farm, called Candy Roaster. The shop went through a period of slight mania over this squash, which is supersweet and bizarrely oblong shaped. One fall, we were obsessed with steaming way more than we needed for this caramel and eating huge chunks of it with olive oil and sea salt, spooning it up off the skin in a weird delirium. The next year, the farm didn't grow it and I've never seen it since, though a former chocolatier, Shana, managed to find some in Denver and bought all she could to be able to have it all winter.

If you can't obtain this extremely hard-to-find variety, don't worry; we've made this caramel with all kinds of squash, and even sweet potatoes. Use any sweet-fleshed squash, such as Kabocha, Hubbard, Sweet Dumpling, Turban, Red Kuri, or Long Island Cheese Pumpkin.

For a garnish, we pipe tempered chocolate into lines and swoops, but this is completely optional.

This caramel makes a large amount, but halving the recipe increases its chances of crystallizing and burning, so you'll just have to enjoy lots of these beauties. Pity.

Makes roughly 100 caramels

1 (1-pound) winter squash

2¼ cups/500 g coconut milk

¾ cup/84 g coconut oil

2 cups/629 g pure maple syrup

2 cups/383 g Cane Syrup (page 96) or organic corn syrup

1 heaping tablespoon/11 g fleur de sel sea salt

½ teaspoon/1 g ground cinnamon

¼ teaspoon/1 g ground cloves

¼ teaspoon/.5 g ground nutmeg

1½ teaspoons/7 g pure vanilla extract

2 teaspoons/10 g cream of tartar

1½ cups/8 ounces/200 g vegan white chocolate

1 pound chocolate, for dipping

1. Steam the squash (do not boil or roast; it will make your puree too watery and too gritty, respectively) until perfectly tender; wash, then hack the squash into big pieces with the skin still on.
2. Scoop out the seeds with a spoon. If you don't have a steamer pot, dollar stores usually sell steamer inserts, or rig one up by setting a colander filled with the squash inside a pot, pouring in water just to come to the bottom of the colander (so it never touches the squash), and putting a lid over everything. Set the water to just simmering (make sure you don't run out of water and burn your pot) and cook for 30 minutes, or until the squash is falling-apart tender. You can't overcook this squash, but undercooking it will make it gritty and sad.
3. Lift out the squash, scoop it away from the skin, and wrap the squash in cheesecloth or just use your hands to squeeze out about half the water you could squeeze out from the squash flesh—don't aggressively remove all the water, or the caramel will burn. Don't stress about this step too much; it'll be okay no matter how you do it. Measure out 250 g (about 1 cup) of the squash puree and save the rest for another use.
4. Combine 1⅛ cups/250 g of the milk with the oil, maple syrup, cane syrup, and salt in a 2- to 4-quart pot. Stir gently, then bring to a boil over medium heat without stirring. While the mixture is cooking, wash down the sides of the pan with a pastry brush dipped in cool water every 10 minutes or so, to prevent sugar crystals from forming on the side of the pot, jumping into the caramel, and making it gritty.
5. Cook over medium-low heat (the mixture should be simmering, but not climbing the sides of the pan) until the caramel registers about 250°F on a candy thermometer. Stir gently once in a while to ensure the caramel doesn't burn.
6. While the caramel is cooking, blend the squash puree and the remaining 1⅛ cups/250 g of milk in a blender. Add the squash mixture and spices to the pot when it reaches about 250°F.
7. Continue to cook until the caramel registers 261°F. If it looks like it's burning before it comes to temperature, remove it from the heat when it's as high as it will go without burning, and proceed with the recipe.
8. Turn off the heat and stir in the vanilla, cream of tartar, and white chocolate with a whisk.
9. Carefully pour the caramel into molds or a prepared pan (see page 114). Let set up for 20 minutes, or until slightly firm, then cover with plastic wrap and freeze.
10. Keep the caramels in the freezer in their molds or pan so they keep their shape. Temper the chocolate (see page 17), and dip the caramels into it, using a dipping fork, regular fork, or your fingers.
11. When the chocolate is set, put the tempered chocolate into a pastry bag and pipe decoratively onto the dipped caramels.

(recipe photo shown on page 92)

riesling rose caramels

....

We made this one in a partnership with our local vegan anarchist winery, Whitecliff Vineyard. Whitecliff's Riesling is soft, rosy, friendly and gentle, with good New York grapes. Because we first made this caramel for Mother's Day 2013, I always associate it with springtime—flowery air and this delicate, ephemeral friend.

Makes 65 caramels

½ cup plus 2 tablespoons/150 g coconut milk

¼ cup/42 g coconut oil

2¼ cups/450 g sugar

6 tablespoons/112 g Cane Syrup (page 96) or organic corn syrup

1 teaspoon/3 g fleur de sel sea salt

½ cup plus 2 tablespoons/125 g Riesling wine

1 vanilla bean, split and scraped

1 tablespoon/14 g pure vanilla extract

1 teaspoon/5 g cream of tartar

2 teaspoons/8 g rose water

1 pound chocolate, for dipping

Garnish: flaky sea salt or fresh or dried rose petals, preferably organically grown

1. Combine the milk, oil, sugar, syrup, and salt in a 4-quart pot. Stir gently, then bring to a boil over medium heat without stirring. While the mixture is cooking, wash down the sides of the pan with a pastry brush dipped in cool water every 10 minutes or so, to prevent sugar crystals from forming on the side of the pot, jumping into the caramel, and making it gritty.
2. Cook over medium-low heat (the mixture should be simmering, but not climbing the sides of the pan) until the caramel registers 240°F on a candy thermometer. Add the wine.
3. Continue to cook until the caramel comes to 265°F.

4. Turn off the heat and stir in the vanilla bean scrapings, vanilla, cream of tartar, and rose water with a whisk.
5. Carefully pour the caramel into molds or a prepared pan (see page 114). Let set up for 20 minutes or until slightly firm, then cover with plastic wrap and freeze.
6. Keep the caramels in the freezer in their molds or pan so they keep their shape. Temper the chocolate (see page 17), and dip the caramels into it, using a dipping fork, regular fork, or your fingers. Garnish with flaky salt or rose petals while the chocolate is wet.

rosemary sea salt caramels

· ·

Babies in the womb developing a William Carlos Williams's taste for plums who'll nonetheless grow up to sneak blue Icees from the full-service station on the Palisades—smallest cup, fill it up one quarter of the way because // whole foods eaten in season organic fair trade local // but blue is patently the best flavor and the cashier is unimpressed at your attempt at purity & the minute the blue hits your veins you're good at something again you didn't know you'd sucked at.

And the rest of the trip up (empty cup already; treatless, HFCS deprived) all you can think is: who in Trump's America takes less Icee than they pay for? Only this chump & what flavor was white, anyway? You'll say pineapple because you have more optimism than I can imagine ever having had but I know the truth and it's Mountain Dew.

Scoop straw

Waxy cup

Blue tongue

Desire.

And basically this is how I want to run my business. Taste memories. Icee got into me, walking past the Circle K, Sharpied Keds melting into hot blacktop of 1988 Phoenix, eyeing the beautiful blue swirling slush, my good mom frowned on bad stuff but somehow it got into me, imprinted—I wanna Pavlov you, flood your senses, Proust madeline you with hot sugar with rosemary stirred in at 261 degrees.

Our chocolate shop opened in 2011 and it's a weird and proud feeling to see New Paltz kids (Wild Earth T-shirts, Mohonk Preserve field trips, tie-dyed gender-nonconforming midlength shaggy hair) expertly asking on tiptoe for a Rosemary Sea Salt Caramel; their friends come to town and they teach them the ways: the Strawberry Balsamic Caramels are good and sour, the Thyme Lemon you'll like, the Rosemary are the best. We're worming in we're worming in, we're Iceeing you.

This little baby, the first caramel we ever made, we still make it every week, filling the shop with the piney smell of rosemary, tray after tray of little squares setting up, shifting quietly from liquid to solid.

Makes 52 caramels

¾ cup/180 g coconut milk

¼ cup/42 g coconut oil

1½ cups/300 g sugar

½ cup/150 g Cane Syrup (page 96) or organic corn syrup

1 tablespoon/8 g fleur de sel sea salt

1 vanilla bean, split and scraped

2 teaspoons/5 g pure vanilla extract

2 tablespoons/4 g ground dried rosemary (measure after grinding if you're grinding, otherwise buy ground rosemary)

2 teaspoons/9 g cream of tartar

1 pound chocolate, for dipping

Garnish: fresh or dried whole rosemary

1. Combine the milk, oil, sugar, syrup, and salt in a 2- to 4-quart pot. Stir gently, then bring to a boil over medium heat without stirring. While the mixture is cooking, wash down the sides of the pan with a pastry brush dipped in cool water every 10 minutes or so, to prevent sugar crystals from forming on the side of the pot, jumping into the caramel, and making it gritty.
2. Cook over medium-low heat (the mixture should be simmering, but not climbing the sides of the pan) until the caramel registers 261°F on a candy thermometer.
3. Turn off the heat and stir in the vanilla bean scrapings, vanilla, rosemary, and cream of tartar with a whisk.
4. Carefully pour the caramel into molds or a prepared pan (see page 114). Let set up for 20 minutes, or until slightly firm, then cover with plastic wrap and freeze.
5. Keep the caramels in the freezer in their molds or pan so they keep their shape. Temper the chocolate (see page 17), and dip the caramels into it, using a dipping fork, regular fork, or your fingers. Garnish with fresh or dried rosemary while the chocolate is wet.

strawberry balsamic caramels

· ·

I started reading Brooks Headley's *Fancy Desserts* about a week before my mom was diagnosed with cancer. My life switched overnight from chocolate production work to caretaking, and *Fancy Desserts* was my relief from increasingly bleak doctors' appointments. I fell for it hard. It was my confectionery *Bell Jar*, I wanted to know it all by heart. When my business partner and I decided to open a New York City retail sweets shop, we already knew we only wanted to be in the East Village, and when we went to look at a dinky storefront on East Ninth Street, half a block down from Brooks's restaurant Superiority Burger, everything felt fated. While we built Confectionery!, Brooks & co. kept bringing us heart-stoppingly perfect little snacks to keep us sated while painting and sanding and hanging wallpaper, and I tried to keep my love for *Fancy Desserts* quiet. It was impossible, and once I outed myself, Brooks and I became pals and I'm so grateful. That dude is weird. I'm glad he's in my life.

One of the many stupidly simple and completely revelatory confectionery techniques I learned from Brooks was vinegar in dessert. Once I started with it, I couldn't stop. And so, these caramels. A classic Italian flavor combination, sweet and fruity and tart and lovely.

These use both strawberry puree and a powder made from freeze-dried strawberries. This double dose of strawberry flavor makes a more complex, ultrafruity caramel with a good texture. To make a powder from freeze-dried strawberries (which are available in most supermarkets and health food stores), grind them in a spice grinder. Leave some strawberries whole as a garnish for the finished caramels.

This caramel has a tendency to burn, so it has instructions to gently stir the pot, unlike almost all other caramel recipes. Because the fruit makes the caramel softer, it also cooks to a much higher temperature than typical caramel recipes.

Makes 50 caramels

1 teaspoon/5 g cream of tartar

½ cup/25 g strawberry powder (from freeze-dried strawberries)

¼ teaspoon freshly ground black pepper

3 tablespoons/24 g white balsamic vinegar

1 cup/240 g coconut milk

¼ cup/42 g coconut oil

1¾ cups/362 g sugar

¾ cup/162 g Cane Syrup (page 96) or organic corn syrup

1 scant tablespoon/8 g fleur de sel sea salt

⅔ cup/137 g strawberry puree (puree thawed frozen or fresh,
     hulled strawberries in a blender—no need to strain)

1 pound chocolate, for dipping

Garnish: freeze-dried strawberries

1. Combine the cream of tartar, strawberry powder, pepper, and vinegar in a small bowl and set aside.
2. Combine the milk, oil, sugar, syrup, and salt in a 2- to 4-quart pot. Stir gently, then bring to a boil over medium heat without stirring. While the mixture is cooking, wash down the sides of the pan with a pastry brush dipped in cool water every 10 minutes or so, to prevent sugar crystals from forming on the side of the pot, jumping into the caramel, and making it gritty.
3. Cook over medium-low heat (the mixture should be simmering, but not climbing the sides of the pan) until the caramel registers 275°F on a candy thermometer. Add the strawberry puree. Slowly, with minimal splashing, stir the pot periodically to avoid burning. Continue to cook until the caramel registers 282°F on a candy thermometer.
4. Turn off the heat and stir in the strawberry powder mixture with a whisk.
5. Carefully pour the caramel into molds or a prepared pan (see page 114). Let set up for 20 minutes, or until slightly firm, then cover with plastic wrap and freeze.
6. Keep the caramels in the freezer in their molds or pan so they keep their shape. Temper the chocolate (see page 17), and dip the caramels into it, using a dipping fork, regular fork, or your fingers. Garnish with freeze-dried strawberries while the chocolate is wet.

thyme preserved lemon sea salt caramels

· ·

The best caramel I've ever made. Candies with three layers of flavor are always my favorite—a Goldilocks number of tastes.

My formula for a great caramel or chocolate bonbon is so foolproof, I have to force myself to not rely on it every time:

Tart element + earthy element + salt. So easy! The tart element can be a vinegar used straight or made into a sweet-sour syrup, a citrus, or a naturally sour herb or spice. The earthy element can be an herb, vegetable puree, smoked thing, or deeply roasted nut. The salt element can be miso or any one of an endless number of fancy salts (or pickle brine or sauerkraut or or or or).

Fran Bigelow of Fran's Chocolates in Seattle began marketing sea salt caramels (a French classic from Brittany for generations) in the 1980s and the universe has opened its endless maw for them in ever-increasing desirousness ever since. I keep creating new caramels and telling myself I won't garnish them with sea salt, but the combination is so heart-achingly good that I keep doing it. I also take great pleasure in squandering precious food cost dollars by ordering an ever-expanding number of interesting sea salts from the Meadow, the specialty salt and chocolate shop in Portland and New York. This caramel uses their sublime sunny yellow lemon-infused sea salt, but regular fleur de sel or any nice chunky salt will work as well.

You can buy preserved lemons, but they're dead easy to make: just salt, citrus, and time (recipe follows). Any citrus will do, too. I buy cases of Meyer lemons when they come into season in the wintertime, typically in that tiny window between the crushing December holiday rush and the crushing Valentine's rush, and put up a few gallons of preserved lemons to use in this caramel all year. You can add spices to these, also: fennel, cinnamon, cloves, anise, coriander, peppercorns, hot chiles, cardamom...so many. I like to keep the flavor neutral so I can adapt them to many different recipes.

Makes 40 caramels

1½ teaspoons/7 g preserved lemon peel (recipe follows)

2 tablespoons/2 g dried thyme

1 teaspoon/5 g pure vanilla extract

1 teaspoon/5 g cream of tartar

½ cup/120 g coconut milk

2 tablespoons/21 g coconut oil

¾ cup plus 2 tablespoons/187 g sugar

¾ cup/200 g Cane Syrup (page 96) or organic corn syrup

1½ teaspoons/5 g fleur de sel sea salt

1 vanilla bean, split and scraped

1 pound chocolate, for dipping

Garnish: lemon-infused sea salt

1. Finely mince the preserved lemon peel and thyme together. Mix with the vanilla and cream of tartar in a small dish and set aside.
2. Combine the milk, oil, sugar, syrup, and salt in a 2- to 4-quart pot. Stir gently, then bring to a boil over medium heat without stirring. While the mixture is cooking, wash down the sides of the pan with a pastry brush dipped in cool water every 10 minutes or so, to prevent sugar crystals from forming on the side of the pot, jumping into the caramel, and making it gritty.
3. Cook over medium-low heat (the mixture should be simmering, but not climbing the sides of the pan) until the caramel registers 261°F on a candy thermometer.
4. Turn off the heat and beat in the lemon mixture and vanilla bean scrapings with a whisk.
5. Carefully pour the caramel into molds or a prepared pan (see page 114). Let set up for 20 minutes, or until slightly firm, then cover with plastic wrap and freeze.
6. Keep the caramels in the freezer in their molds or pan so they keep their shape. Temper the chocolate (see page 17), and dip the caramels into it, using a dipping fork, regular fork, or your fingers. Garnish with lemon-infused sea salt while the chocolate is wet.

Preserved Lemons

Lemons, however many you want, 5 or 10 or 15 or 100

Sea salt, a cheap kind, a lot of it

Special equipment: wide-mouth quart-size jars, 1 jar per 5 to 8 lemons, depending on size of lemons

1. Wash the jars well. No need to sterilize them, but if you have a dishwasher, you can run them through on the hottest setting. Sprinkle some salt, about ½ teaspoon, into each jar.
2. Separate out and reserve about a quarter of your lemons to juice. On each remaining lemon, make four to six slits from top to bottom with a sharp paring knife. Stuff as much sea salt as you can into each slit. If a lemon splits open, it's okay, but try to avoid it. Obviously, wear gloves if you have any cuts on your hands, to avoid rubbing literal salt into your wounds.
3. Pack the lemons into your jars as tightly as you can. Really stuff them in good; keep pushing and stuffing and put some cut lemons rolled in salt to fill up the spaces where whole lemons won't fit.
4. Juice the reserved lemons. Fill up the jars with lemon juice to completely cover the salt-stuffed lemons.
5. Screw the caps on the jars and label them with the date. Let sit in a cool, dark area, such as the back of a cupboard or a basement, and flip them upside down a few times every week or whenever you think about it. You can use them after a month, but I like to let them sit for at least 3 and preferably 6 months.
6. Preserved lemons are good almost anywhere you'd use a little lemon and a little salt: vinaigrettes, vegetable stews, rice, ice-cream sundaes, and so on. Rinse the lemons before using, to cut down on the intense saltiness, or don't. The saline lemon syrup left over after the lemons have been used makes an excellent "starter" for your next batch of preserved citrus, or put a little in a martini, salad dressing, lemonade, or Rosh Hashanah tzimmes.

Caramel Candies Wrapped in Waxed Paper

The flavor of these caramels is muted or erased when enrobed in dark chocolate, so we don't coat them. Instead, we cook them to a slightly higher temperature and wrap them in waxed confectionery paper, which you can get in kitchen supply stores or online (sometimes labeled as "confectionery twisting paper."). Regular waxed paper works just fine, too; you'll just need to cut it to size.

Springtime Spruce Lemon Caramels (page 162)

bridge to paris pepper caramels

· ·

I love farmers. Farmers are lunatics, like food professionals.

Like food, farming is a job you don't devote your life to unless you have no hope of seeing friends nine months out of the year; maintaining soft, unblemished hands; establishing healthy retirement savings; or working normal working hours. Farmers don't think they're interesting, but they're all fascinating.

Also, they bring you presents. What chocolatier doesn't covet the freshest spring spinach or an heirloom pumpkin as a treat? Sugar people are always desperate for savories. For that matter, what farmer doesn't want a chocolate? Soulmates. Most of the farmers I know are women and they are all indestructible ribbons of energy and light. Erin, Sam, Jessica, Kyra, Megan, Lydia, Jenna, Allison—I'd trust these women with my life, for sure.

Erin and Sam have their own farm and are the primary produce suppliers for our café, Lagusta's Luscious Commissary!, two blocks from Lagusta's Luscious chocolate HQ. Erin and Sam introduced me to this excellent sweet pepper, which has its own great backstory. Another local farm I love, Phillies Bridge Farm, had originally grown it out and brought it to the attention of Ken and Doug, friends of mine who run the Hudson Valley Seed Company. Over the years we've collaborated on lots of chocolate-, produce-, and seed-related projects, and I love Ken and Doug deeply for their passionate politics and exhausted small business-owner hearts. I love this pepper because of all these connections, too, and made this caramel to celebrate these webs of friendship.

The Bridge to Paris pepper is shockingly, outstandingly sweet. It cries to be made into dessert. Unless you live in the mid-Hudson Valley and it's July, or unless you grow it yourself from seeds provided by the Hudson Valley Seed Company, you probably aren't going to be able to use this exact variety. Luckily, a regular old red sweet pepper works just fine. We freeze Bridge to Paris pepper puree when it's in season for this caramel, so if your CSA or farmers' market has a glut of summery, ultraripe red sweet peppers, do the same and save the puree for when you want to make this caramel. The sweetness of roasted peppers matches caramel flawlessly. Don't think of them as a vegetable, because when they're roasted and pureed, they are sweeter than many fruits.

Makes 50 caramels

2 large fresh red bell peppers (about 1½ pounds)

Olive oil, for roasting

Salt and freshly ground black pepper, for roasting

1 cup/240 g coconut milk

¼ cup/42 g coconut oil

1¾ cups/362 g sugar

½ cup/150 g Cane Syrup (page 96) or organic corn syrup

1 tablespoon/8 g fleur de sel sea salt

1 teaspoon/5 g cream of tartar

1. Roast and puree the peppers: Preheat your oven to 400°F. Devein and core the peppers, but otherwise leave them whole. Toss with a little olive oil and salt and pepper and roast on a sheet pan until blackened in spots and evenly roasted, 20 to 30 minutes, depending on your oven. Immediately transfer, with the pan juices, to a bowl. Cover with plastic wrap and let sit for 10 minutes or so. The peel should slip off the peppers easily. Discard the peel and puree the pepper flesh and juices in a food processor. Weigh out 100 g (about 3.5 ounces) of pureed pepper. (Use the rest for red pepper soup or stirring into hummus or fancy baby food.)

2. Combine the milk, oil, sugar, syrup, and salt in a 2- to 4-quart pot. Stir gently, then bring to a boil over medium heat without stirring. While the mixture is cooking, wash down the sides of the pan with a pastry brush dipped in cool water every 10 minutes or so, to prevent sugar crystals from forming on the side of the pot, jumping into the caramel, and making it gritty.

3. Cook over medium-low heat (the mixture should be simmering, but not climbing the sides of the pan) until the caramel registers roughly 245°F, then stir in the pepper puree. Continue to cook until the caramel registers 262°F on a candy thermometer.

4. Turn off the heat and stir in the cream of tartar with a whisk.

5. Carefully pour the caramel into molds or a prepared pan (see page 114). Let set up for 20 minutes, or until slightly firm, then cover with plastic wrap and freeze.

6. While frozen, wrap in confectionery paper or waxed paper.

caramelized onion and chipotle caramels

· ·

We make a truffle with these same flavors, but the onion and spice shine through in different ways in this caramel. They're equally strange and wonderful. The sweetness of the slow-cooked onion matches caramel nicely, and the chipotle adds layers of smokiness and cuts through all the toasty caramelized flavors so they don't become cloying.

Makes 38 caramels

Scant 1 cup/222 g coconut milk

¼ cup/42 g coconut oil

1½ cups/355 g sugar

½ cup/162 g Cane Syrup (page 96) or organic corn syrup

1 tablespoon/16 g sea salt

6 tablespoons/87 g pureed caramelized onion (page 59)

1 teaspoon/5 g cream of tartar

¾ teaspoon/2 g chipotle chile powder

Pinch of cayenne pepper

1. Combine the milk, oil, sugar, syrup, and salt in a 2- to 4-quart pot. Stir gently, then bring to a boil over medium heat without stirring. While the mixture is cooking, wash down the sides of the pan with a pastry brush dipped in cool water every 10 minutes or so, to prevent sugar crystals from forming on the side of the pot, jumping into the caramel, and making it gritty.
2. Cook over medium-low heat (the mixture should be simmering, but not climbing the sides of the pan) until the caramel registers 259°F on a candy thermometer.
3. Turn off the heat and stir in the remaining ingredients with a whisk.
4. Carefully pour the caramel into molds or a prepared pan (see page 114). Let set up for 20 minutes, or until slightly firm, then cover with plastic wrap and freeze.
5. While frozen, wrap in confectionery paper or waxed paper.

carrot coriander caramels

· ·

Carrots are sweet! And make a good caramel. And go perfectly with coriander, which adds fruity warmth and savor. You can use regular supermarket ground coriander, or you can toast and grind your own. The former is fine, the latter is spectacular. Toast a few tablespoons of whole coriander in a dry pan until it's one shade darker and your kitchen is filled with a gorgeous coriander aroma, then let it cool and grind it in a spice grinder. You'll have more than you need for this recipe, but you can sprinkle it on roasted vegetables, pasta, put it in homemade pickles, make salad dressings with it, or add it to your caramelized onions.

This caramel cooks to a much higher temperature, 268°F, than most because the carrot juice makes the mixture softer, so the sugar needs to be cooked to a higher degree to set up properly.

Makes about 35 caramels

⅔ cup/150 g coconut milk

2 tablespoons/28 g coconut oil

1 cup plus 2 tablespoons/240 g sugar

¼ cup plus 1 tablespoon/108 g Cane Syrup (page 96) or organic corn syrup

1 tablespoon/8 g fleur de sel sea salt

⅓ cup/90 g fresh carrot juice

1 tablespoon/5 g ground toasted coriander seeds

1 vanilla bean, split and scraped

1 teaspoon/5 g pure vanilla extract

1 teaspoon/5 g cream of tartar

1. Combine the milk, oil, sugar, syrup, and salt in a 2- to 4-quart pot. Stir gently, then bring to a boil over medium heat without stirring. While the mixture is cooking, wash down the sides of the pan with a pastry brush dipped in cool water every 10 minutes or so, to prevent sugar crystals from forming on the side of the pot, jumping into the caramel, and making it gritty.

2. Cook over medium-low heat (the mixture should be simmering, but not climbing the sides of the pan) until the caramel registers 250°F on a candy thermometer. Add the carrot juice and cook until the caramel comes to 268°F.
3. Turn off the heat and stir in the remaining ingredients with a whisk.
4. Carefully pour the caramel into molds or a prepared pan (see page 114). Let set up for 20 minutes, or until slightly firm, then cover with plastic wrap and freeze.
5. While frozen, wrap in confectionery paper or waxed paper.

local licorice

....

I had this weird slow-motion nervous breakdown the summer of 2017. I'd been in a relationship for twenty years that was slowly (and then not so slowly) eroding, the wild stress from opening two businesses a few months after a year spent caring for my mother as she succumbed to pancreatic cancer was catching up to me, my brother was homeless for a bit (long story!), I tumbled into an intense romantic entanglement that ended in ways that took the breath out of me for months, and my cats kept dying. Also I wasn't so fond of the president. Weird summer.

The only thing I could really do was work on this licorice recipe. One of our chocolatiers, Chloe, a true Goth candywitch supreme and the coolest woman in our town by several magnitudes, had made a pilgrimage to Norway earlier in the year and I asked her to look for salty licorice. She couldn't find any that was vegan, so I decided to make some.

It took a long time, because most of my days were spent taking annoying depression-crying naps in my car.

By November, I was okay. I got my first tattoo, got a sweet new boyfriend, moved into a gorgeous new house, my brother stabilized, I started meditating for real, and felt like myself again. Most thrilling of all, from a sugar standpoint at least, is this licorice.

It might be the most annoying recipe in the book, but it's pretty dang mind-blowing. This recipe makes the ne plus ultra licorice, and as such it uses every variety of anise- and fennel-tasting edible around. You can leave out the sassafras powder if you can't find it. You can also leave out the absinthe. I recommend making this when farmers' market fennel is in season, so you can brag on social media about your #locallicorice. And it's gluten-free, which makes it extra special, since most licorice has gluten. We use teff flour instead of wheat flour. It's available in almost all health food stores. Charcoal powder, also available in health food stores, is used instead of artificial black food coloring.

The base of this caramel is a cauldron-full of glorious, deep black, glossy fennel syrup that is also useful for:

- Using as the base for seltzer- or alcohol-based drinks
- Drizzling on ice cream or baked goods
- Making into ice cream
- Getting all over children's faces and bodies
- Halloween-related everything

The syrup will keep for months in the freezer and for two months in the refrigerator. I recommend tripling it so you can be ready to make licoricey confections, drinks, and more quickly.

I can't promise that this recipe will cure a nervous breakdown, but it does seem to have some special magic. Go for it.

Makes 45 caramels

2 cups/443 g coconut milk

½ cup/84 g coconut oil

3½ cups/1,050 g strained Fennel Syrup (recipe follows)

3 tablespoons/18 g fleur de sel sea salt

9 tablespoons/100 g absinthe

1 heaping tablespoon charcoal powder

¼ cup/25 g teff flour

2 teaspoons/8 g anise extract (optional)

1 teaspoon/5 g cream of tartar

1. Combine the milk, oil, fennel syrup, salt, absinthe, and charcoal in a 2- to 4-quart pot. Stir gently, then bring to a boil over medium heat without stirring. While the mixture is cooking, wash down the sides of the pan with a pastry brush dipped in cool water every 10 minutes or so, to prevent sugar crystals from forming on the side of the pot, jumping into the caramel, and making it gritty.
2. Cook over medium-low heat (the mixture should be simmering, but not climbing the sides of the pan) until the caramel registers 240°F on a candy thermometer. Add the teff flour and gently stir to incorporate, being sure not to splash on the sides of the pot.
3. When the caramel comes to 259°F, remove from the heat and stir in the anise extract and cream of tartar.
4. Carefully pour the caramel into molds or a prepared pan (see page 114). Let set up for 20 minutes, or until slightly firm, then cover with plastic wrap and freeze.
5. While frozen, wrap in confectionery paper or waxed paper.

Fennel Syrup

Makes 3 cups syrup

¼ cup/18 g whole fennel seeds

¼ cup/25 g whole star anise

4 cups/450 g chopped, cored fennel, from 2 large or
  3 medium fennel bulbs (about 1½ pounds)

3 cups/600 g sugar

3¼ cups/750 g water

¼ cup/4 g charcoal powder

¼ cup/4 g sassafras powder or sassafras leaves (more is okay, too)

1. Place the fennel seeds and star anise in a dry pan and toast over medium heat until one shade darker and fragrant. Let cool and grind in a spice grinder.
2. Place all the remaining syrup ingredients plus the ground fennel and anise mixture in a 4-quart pot, bring to a boil, then lower the heat to a gentle simmer. Cook, covered, until the fennel has sunk to the bottom and a heavy syrup has formed, 2 hours or so.
3. Let the syrup sit overnight, then strain.

springtime spruce lemon caramels

••

These are a springy version of our Thyme Preserved Lemon Sea Salt Caramels (page 146), but gentler, more lemon-forward and spruce-prominent. We don't coat these in chocolate; instead this spring ephemeral is wrapped in waxed paper so its delicate May vibes don't get corrupted by muscular 66%. Personally, I think it rules. The spruce in it is so gentle, never overwhelming, it just adds a hint of forest flavor.

If you don't live in a spruce region or can't forage some, you can make these with *culinary-grade* spruce essential oil (check the label to be sure of this), which is available in most health food stores. To substitute spruce oil for ground spruce, add 10 drops of it along with the vanilla at the end, instead of with the ground spruce as indicated in the recipe.

If you don't have and don't want to make or buy preserved lemon, omit it, for a purely spruce caramel that's lovely in a different way.

In this caramel we use sea salt infused with lemon from the Meadow, a specialty salt shop in Portland and New York City, but you can use regular sea salt, too, just use a smidge less.

Makes 30 caramels

½ cup/120 g coconut milk

2 tablespoons/21 g coconut oil

¾ cup/181 g sugar

¼ cup/81 g Cane Syrup (page 96) or organic corn syrup

3 tablespoons/20 g fresh spruce tips, ground to a fine powder (see headnote)

1½ teaspoons/4 g lemon fleur de sel sea salt

1 tablespoon/11 g preserved lemon (page 149), very finely minced

½ vanilla bean, split and scraped

1½ teaspoons/7 g pure vanilla extract

¼ teaspoon/2 g culinary-grade lemon oil (not extract or essential oil)

½ teaspoon/3 g cream of tartar

1. Combine the milk, oil, sugar, syrup, spruce, and salt in a 2- to 4-quart pot. (If using spruce oil, add with the vanilla at the end.) Stir gently, then bring to a boil over medium heat without stirring. While the mixture is cooking, wash down the sides of the pan with a pastry brush dipped in cool water every 10 minutes or so, to prevent sugar crystals from forming on the side of the pot, jumping into the caramel, and making it gritty.
2. Cook over medium-low heat (the mixture should be simmering, but not climbing the sides of the pan) until the caramel registers 265°F on a candy thermometer.
3. Turn off the heat and stir in the remaining ingredients with a whisk.
4. Carefully pour the caramel into molds or a prepared pan (see page 114). Let set up for 20 minutes, or until slightly firm, then cover with plastic wrap and freeze.
5. While frozen, wrap in confectionery paper or waxed paper.

(recipe photo shown on page 150)

white miso and black sesame caramels

....

I went to culinary school in New York City, in Chelsea at what was then called the Natural Gourmet Cookery School. It was 2000, a fresh new millennium, and I had just moved to New Jersey, just twenty minutes via the bus stop on my corner to Port Authority. I was in New York ("the city," as my housemates quickly taught me to say) six days a week. I had graduated from college in Rochester a month before and had been to the city exactly once before I somehow managed to get a job as an office assistant in the art department at Simon and Schuster, in Rockefeller Center. I'd shown up for the interview with a Mary Tyler Moore-esque wig, to hide my dyed purple hair. I thrifted some decent shoes and put on a bra and got the job. I was elated. For a girl from Phoenix, working in midtown Manhattan was impossibly glamorous. Everyone went out to lunch! And then went shopping! My student-loans-plus-culinary-school-tuition didn't allow such pleasures, so I wore the same three questionably office-appropriate outfits over and over and marveled at the $9 Così sandwiches my co-workers ate. I was so intensely frugal that I didn't allow myself to take the subway unless my destination was more than fifty blocks away. Such ironclad rules allowed me to put myself through culinary school in one year, and had the bonus effect of teaching me Manhattan geography.

I loved the old-fashioned name "Natural Gourmet Cookery School," and I loved the school, though I was such an uptight kid that I often had severe stomach cramps before class, so nervous that I'd have to display my subpar knife skills in front of everyone, or improvise a sauce or filling. I shouldn't have worried. No French-style discipline, no pot throwing. I made an awful lot of gomasio, the simple sesame seed and sea salt condiment, at the Natural Gourmet. Gomasio was billed as a quasi-miracle food, curing headaches brought on by too many "yin foods" (sugar), alleviating hangovers, improving digestion, promoting energy.

This caramel is my homage to my macrobiotic culinary roots—in a winking way, since macrobiotics is vehemently antisugar. Running a business based on sugar feels thrillingly transgressive and rebellious—and I still eat a tablespoon of gomasio if I have a headache brought on by excessive tasting in the shop. Yin and yang.

You can make this caramel with any miso; the flavor will be slightly different with each variety. The miso and sesame oil make this more than a typical salted caramel; the flavors are deeper and earthier and richer.

Makes 45 caramels

1 cup/240 g coconut milk

¼ cup/42 g coconut oil

1 cup/200 g sugar

¾ cup/217 g Cane Syrup (page 96) or organic corn syrup

¼ teaspoon/1 g sea salt

3 tablespoons/23 g sesame oil

2 tablespoons/33 g soy red miso

1 teaspoon/5 g cream of tartar

2 tablespoons/12 g gomasio (recipe follows)

1. Combine all the ingredients, except the cream of tartar and gomasio, in a 2- to 4-quart pot. Whisk to dissolve the miso. Bring to a boil over medium heat without stirring. While the mixture is cooking, wash down the sides of the pan with a pastry brush dipped in cool water every 10 minutes or so, to prevent sugar crystals from forming on the side of the pot, jumping into the caramel, and making it gritty.
2. Cook over medium-low heat (the mixture should be simmering, but not climbing the sides of the pan) until the caramel registers 263°F on a candy thermometer.
3. Turn off the heat and stir in the cream of tartar with a whisk.
4. Carefully pour the caramel into molds or a prepared pan (see page 114). Sprinkle the gomasio evenly over the top of the caramel in a thick layer. Let set up for 20 minutes, or until slightly firm, then cover with plastic wrap and freeze.
5. Wrap in confectionery paper or waxed paper.

Gomasio

You can make gomasio with white sesame seeds, black sesame seeds, or a combination of the two. We use black sesame seeds. You can just mix sea salt into sesame seeds and call it a day, but washing the seeds and toasting them together with the salt pulls the flavors together in a much tastier way. I can't write or think about gomasio without my mouth watering; is that weird?

1 cup/150 g black sesame seeds

½ teaspoon/3 g sea salt

1. Wash the sesame seeds by immersing in a container of water, then lifting out.
2. Put them in a dry pan with the salt.
3. Toast over medium heat, stirring often, until the sesame seeds are dry, roughly 10 minutes.
4. Store the gomasio at room temperature for up to 2 weeks, or refrigerate for up to a month.

Miscellaneous Caramels

Pauline's Caramelized Tofu (page 172)

galapagos turtles

· ·

The jewel in our caramel crown. I think about these turtles a lot. We all do, all of us Lagusta's Luscious people. We're always selling out of them, so we have to. A lot of turtles out in the world are just blobs of caramel with some nuts stuck higgledy-piggledy into them and another blob of chocolate sandwiching everything together. Our turtles are shapely, their bodies, like our own, all slightly different but equally tantalizing. We take a lot of time with them—it's a full-time job for one person to keep up with turtle production, and how lovely, to provide jobs in my community toasting nuts and stretching caramel into Maggie Simpson curves that are tucked just so, dipping them into tempered chocolate to fashion their little brown jumpsuits, blanketing them with good flaky salt, the whole deal. Then doing it all again tomorrow.

Makes about 35 turtles

¼ cup/42 g coconut oil

2 cups packed/350 g light brown sugar (even better is half light and
    half dark brown sugar, but don't stress about it; it works either way)

½ cup/160 g Cane Syrup (page 96) or organic corn syrup

1 cup plus ⅓ cup/313 g coconut milk

½ teaspoon/3 g sea salt

1½ teaspoons/7 g pure vanilla extract

1½ teaspoon/8 g cream of tartar

4½ cups/455 g pecans

½ pound chocolate, for dipping

Garnish: fleur de sel or any nice flaky sea salt

1. Preheat the oven to 375°F. Line two half sheet pans (18 by 13 inches) with parchment paper and set aside.
2. Combine the oil, brown sugar, syrup, milk, and salt in a 4-quart pot. Bring to a boil over medium-high heat.

3. Stir gently, then bring to a boil over medium heat without stirring. While the mixture is cooking, wash down the sides of the pan with a pastry brush dipped in cool water every 10 minutes or so, to prevent sugar crystals from forming on the side of the pot, jumping into the caramel, and making it gritty.

4. Cook over medium-low heat (the mixture should be simmering, but not climbing the sides of the pan) until the caramel registers 257°F on a candy thermometer.

5. Turn off the heat and stir in the vanilla and cream of tartar with a whisk.

6. While the caramel is cooking, toast the pecans on a dry pan in the oven until they are two shades darker, fragrant, and deeply toasted, about 10 minutes. Remove from the oven and set aside to cool.

7. When the caramel comes to temperature, pour out onto one of the prepared sheet pans, then let cool at room temperature until firm enough to cut.

8. Cut a 1-inch-long strip off the short end of the caramel, using a pizza wheel or knife. Stretch the strip until it fits on the second sheet pan diagonally. If the caramel won't stretch, set your oven to its lowest setting and melt the caramel on the sheet pan in it until it's pliable, checking every few minutes. It should be hot enough to work with but not so hot that it burns you. Most likely a microwave would make this process easier, but I'm that annoying person who's never used a microwave, so here's how we do it.

9. When you have a nice pliable strip, cut it into 2-inch lengths to make eight caramel rectangles. Press four pecans onto each corner of each rectangle, to make limbs. Press one pecan between the two leg pecans along a short side, for the head. Repeat until you have about thirty-five turtles. Freeze the turtles in a food storage container lined with parchment paper, with layers of parchment paper between each layer of turtles.

10. Continue making turtles with all of the caramel. Remember to put each strip-worth of turtles into the freezer (if you leave them out for too long, they'll start to lose their shape) with parchment paper beneath and on top of them, so they don't stick together.

11. When the turtles are frozen (about 1 hour, though they'll keep in the freezer for months), temper the chocolate (see page 17) and pour it into a tall container. You want a container just wide enough to fit a turtle. Line a half sheet pan (18 by 13 inches) with parchment paper and have handy a container of flaky sea salt, for garnishing the turtles.

12. Working quickly (so the chocolate doesn't set up), hold each turtle by its head-pecan and dip into the tempered chocolate up to its neck. Shake off excess chocolate back into the container of tempered chocolate, then set the turtle on the lined sheet pan. Grasping the naked pecan turtle head, slide it downward so the back of the head gets coated with a little chocolate. Sprinkle the wet body of the turtle generously with flaky salt.

pauline's caramelized tofu

My mom was (1) the best person to have ever walked this earth, and (2) not much of a cook. She would probably dispute both these charges. She made up for a lack of innate cooking ability by taking fantastically enthusiastic whacks at recipes, to often interesting effect. Like many people who don't cook much, this didn't stop her from having wildly specific food preferences. She loved, in order, (1) saucy foods; (2) burnt foods; (3) creamy foods; (4) sauces; (5) sweet foods; (6) more sauces, please. Never did a human ever love wet food as much as Pauline Dubkin Yearwood. Once, near the end of her life, one of our chocolatiers, Shana, gave her a package from the doughnut of the month club she subscribed to (vegans!) and Pauline was so excited. Vegans (and my mother was vegan for over twenty years) are always excited about doughnuts. My mom took a bite, and I could see the need for some sort of saucy accompaniment in her eyes. She looked right at me and dunked it into the bowl of pho I had just picked up for her. "Pho-nut!" She said to me, triumphantly, and I just laughed and didn't tell her that pho wasn't pronounced like she thought it was.

She made this caramelized tofu recipe a lot. It's sweet and saucy, so it was a natural fit. It's not her recipe, but I associate it with her because of her love for it. I used to make it all the time for the meal delivery service I ran for nine years, but it's originally from Deborah Madison's excellent *Vegetarian Cooking for Everyone*, a heavy book I worked my way through in the early 2000s like it was a textbook, which it was. My recipe is fairly modified, the original is perfect in a different way. This formulation works for all kinds of vegetables, too. It feels defiant—caramel for dinner!—because it is. Who cares?

At our café, our house soy sauce is organic gluten-free tamari, but you can use shoyu or Bragg's Liquid Aminos or whatever floats your boat, fermented soy-wise.

Makes 4 servings

1 pound firm or extra-firm tofu

Grapeseed or other vegetable oil, for frying

Sea salt

¼ cup/60 g tamari or shoyu or other soy sauce

6 tablespoons/75 g granulated sugar or light brown sugar

1. Line a plate with paper towels and set aside.
2. Press the tofu (on a tray or platter, blanketed by paper towels) under a heavy weight for an hour or so. Or don't. Pressing dries out your tofu and makes it fry better, but if you don't have time or inclination, you'll still be fine.
3. Cut the tofu into whatever shape you prefer. I usually do a medium dice kind of a thing.
4. Heat a few tablespoons of oil in a 9-inch skillet and fry the tofu in it when it's nice and hot. Don't stir too much; let it get browned on each side before you turn it, about 5 minutes, then use a good turner with a thin metal edge (something you'd use for pancakes) to confidently scrape it up from the bottom and turn. When all sides are golden brown, remove the pan from the heat, transfer the tofu to paper towels to drain, and sprinkle with sea salt.
5. Stir together the tamari and sugar in a small bowl.
6. In a clean pan, heat a tablespoon or two more of oil over medium heat. Add the tamari mixture and the tofu. Toss well and simmer for a few minutes, until the tofu is syrupy and lovely looking. Add some water if it looks like your caramel is getting too browned.
7. Remove from the heat and let the tofu cool in the syrup for a few minutes before serving.

Heathen Toffee (page 182)

a few more degrees: toffee and hard candy

You've made a lot of caramel by now. Or you just skipped to this section. Either way. Here's a secret: toffee is easier than caramel!

The only real difference between regular caramel and toffee and hard candies is temperature. Higher temperatures make a harder confection. Easy. Screwing up these candies is actually harder than screwing up caramel candies, which are dependent on fairly specific temperatures for their chew and softness. If your toffee cooks to a higher temperature than indicated, it's extra crispy and nice—unless, of course, it starts burning.

Toffee tends to be a little leaner than caramel, using water instead of or in addition to coconut milk, for a more pure, crunchy taste unclouded by soft milky caramel flavors. Toffee is also easier to manipulate into bite-size pieces than caramel. Instead of cutting it into bites, just smash the big sheet of it and eat the jagged shards. (Or wrap a hammer in a paper towel [we put a glove on ours; it's adorable] and delicately smash it up.)

Unlike caramels, toffees and hard candies always always *always* need to be refrigerated (unless you live in a magical world of 0 percent humidity and a consistent 65°F temperature) to maintain their best texture and crispness. Caramel should never be refrigerated; it's best at room temperature. Cold caramel can crack a tooth. But toffee needs to be cold, lest it get soggy and soft. Be sure to store it in a tightly sealed container.

Try not to make toffee on a superhumid day; it'll be stickier.

It might be a good idea to check out "About the Recipes" (page 14) for notes about pot size and recipe measurements before jumping into these.

cough drops

· ·

I never get to make this recipe for the dumb candy shop I run because we always need to focus on "things that make money to be able to run payroll" instead of "things that include wild-foraged herbs and are made in small batches and do not sell well." I'm real psyched about this whole "writing a cookbook thing" mostly because finally we can make cough drops again. This recipe is super versatile! And actually helps a sore throat, I promise.

You can shape your cough drops in a few ways. The easiest way is to pour them out onto a parchment- or silicone mat–lined half sheet pan like toffee, let them firm up at room temperature, then smash them into something resembling bite-size pieces. The resulting shards of glass aren't "drops," but they still work perfectly fine. Or pour them into a silicone mold, as specified for caramel candies. You'll need roughly twenty cavities for this recipe.

These are a caramel candy made from a tea that is cooked to a really high temperature. Make your tea with whatever herbs you want. Or you can use a few drops of equivalent culinary-grade oils, but the flavor of the actual herbs and seeds and roots makes a really delicious cough drop and I'm convinced makes you healthier, too. Feel free to swap out the following ingredients with your favorite sore throat potion. You can use any combination of dried echinacea, licorice root, ginger, cinnamon, slippery elm bark powder, cloves, turmeric, rose petals, or marshmallow root. Or just use an equivalent amount of tea marketed for sore throats. You can go really deep into this world of making quasi-healthy candies. Feel free to call them pastilles, if you want.

The important constant is the peppermint extract. It covers up any weird flavors and cleans out your sinuses. Extract strength varies widely by brand, so if you make this and it's a little weak, add a bunch more peppermint extract next time. The worst thing that could happen would be that your cough drops are a little too soft from the extra liquid, and that's okay. Make them nice and pepperminty.

If these crystallize, they're still okay. Because they're sort of medicine, a different texture than candy is just fine. Just go with it.

Makes 20 to 50 cough drops, depending on how they're molded

2 tablespoons/3 g dried sage, which helps you sweat it out

1 tablespoon/4 g fennel seeds, which soothes your throat

1½ teaspoons/7 g fenugreek seeds, which reduce inflammation

1 tablespoon/5 g juniper seeds, which have a nice woodsy flavor and help fight infection

1 tablespoon/2 g dried chamomile, which is soothing (chamomile tea bags, opened up, work just fine)

2 cups boiling water

½ cup/100 g sugar

Heaping ¼ cup/100 g Cane Syrup (page 96) or organic corn syrup

½ teaspoon/5 g cream of tartar

1 tablespoon/12 g peppermint extract

All-natural food coloring, if desired (a drop or two of green is nice)

Confectioners' sugar, for tossing

1. Lightly grind the sage, fennel, fenugreek, juniper, and chamomile— the aromatics—in a mortar and pestle, or very lightly pulse in a spice grinder. Lacking either, put them in a resealable plastic bag and run over them with a rolling pin until they're a little broken up.
2. Make a strong tea placing the aromatics in a small strainer set over a shallow bowl and pouring the boiling water over them. Cover the bowl with a pot lid and steep for 15 minutes.
3. Prepare to mold your cough drops as directed in the headnote.
4. Combine the tea mixture, sugar, and syrup in a 4-quart pot. Stir gently, then bring to a boil over medium heat without stirring. While the mixture is cooking, wash down the sides of the pan with a pastry brush dipped in cool water every 10 minutes or so, to prevent sugar crystals from forming on the side of the pot, jumping into the mixture, and making it gritty.
5. Cook over medium-low heat (the mixture should be simmering, but not climbing the sides of the pan) until the mixture registers 261°F on a candy thermometer.
6. Add the cream of tartar, peppermint extract, and food coloring, if using, then stir and quickly pour into the molds.
7. When the cough drops are firm, remove from the molds and put into a lidded container filled halfway with confectioners' sugar. Shake to coat the cough drops, transfer to a strainer, shake off excess sugar, and store in an airtight container in the refrigerator.
8. If your cough drops get sticky, repeat the confectioners' sugar shaking procedure.

kate's strawberry seltzer fizz candies

Vegans love junk food, cats love walking on your face in the middle of the night, and punks love seltzer: these are things I know. Kate is a seltz connoisseur in the special way of vegan sober punks, which means she is very deep into her bubbles.

How do I explain Kate to you in a way that will make you love her as I do, and want to make these candies in her honor? To start, we dated in a polyamorous way for three years, and we still work together, if that says anything about what a special human she is.

Kate keeps us steady. She is also utterly unswayed by my repeated attempts to shove a percentage of the business at her, knowing that it would mean more work nightmares than she already has, less of an ability to go on summer tours with her various bands and pursue her many zine- and art-related projects during slow months than she has now. Smart one, that one. She's one of those people who make our world incomparably rich, whose vision and true punk heart make us much greater.

This recipe is a great introduction to the world of pulled sugar candies. The only real trick is to work as quickly as possible. It will also be helpful to have on hand clean kitchen scissors whose blades have been lightly oiled with coconut or vegetable oil, and disposable vinyl gloves.

Citric acid, strawberry extract, and all-natural food coloring are available online or in some supermarkets.

Makes around 5 ounces/about 30 candies

Fizz

1 teaspoon/5 g citric acid
1 teaspoon/5 g baking soda
2 teaspoons/8 g confectioners' sugar

Hard candy base

½ cup/100 g granulated sugar

3½ tablespoons/60 g Cane Syrup (page 96) or organic corn syrup

¼ cup/68 g water

¼ teaspoon strawberry extract

All-natural red food coloring

1. Line a half sheet pan (18 by 13 inches) with a sheet of parchment paper or a silicone baking mat.
2. Combine all the fizz ingredients in a small, dry bowl. Any moisture will activate the fizziness (which you want to do only when eating these), so be sure all utensils and bowls are dry.
3. Prepare the candy base: Combine the sugar, syrup, and water in a 2- to 4-quart pot and bring to a boil, without stirring. Cook over medium-low heat. While the mixture is cooking, wash down the sides of the pan with a pastry brush dipped in cool water every 10 minutes or so, to prevent sugar crystals from forming on the side of the pot, jumping into the mixture, and making it gritty.
4. Cook over medium-low heat (the mixture should be simmering, but not climbing the sides of the pan) until the mixture registers 305°F on a candy thermometer. The temperature will climb quickly after it reaches 270°F or so.
5. Remove from the heat, and gently whisk in the strawberry extract and a few drops of red food coloring.
6. Working as quickly as you can, pour out the sugar mixture into a rectangular shape on the lined sheet pan. Sprinkle the fizz mixture over it in a neat line lengthwise along its center. Wearing disposable vinyl gloves, roll up the rectangle like a cinnamon roll with the fizz mixture in the middle. Quickly fold the roll over on itself a few times the other direction, to evenly mix the fizz into itself. Don't overmix; just fold it over onto itself a few times, then quickly pull the mass into a long, thin rope, twisting as you go. Cut with oiled scissors into 1-inch-long candies.
7. If at any point the candy sets up and becomes brittle and not pliable, quickly warm it in an oven set to 250°F until it's workable again. Warming your sugar dough will make it hotter, so use extreme caution when pulling it.

heathen toffee

Nearly a decade on, and the name still cracks me up. My friend Aaron named it; thanks, Aaron!

The toffee, though. I made it twelve times in a row to get it right. Tiny changes every time. So now, you only need to make it once and it'll be the buttery crispy dream-toffee you've been wanting all these years since you watched that one documentary about how cows aren't happy to give you their milk.

The key is the crispiness. No one wants toffee with no snap. What we're always telling new worker bees about it is this: you think you're going to burn it. But 99 percent of the time, if there's a problem, it's that it's not crispy enough. Err on the side of burning it.

Makes 2 pounds toffee

1¾ cups/226 g almonds
2½ cups/500 g sugar
¾ cup/177 g water
¾ cup/170 g coconut milk
5 tablespoons/65 g coconut oil
Scant ¾ cup/194 g Cane Syrup (page 96) or organic corn syrup
1½ teaspoons/10 g sea salt
1 teaspoon/7 g baking soda
1 tablespoon/14 g pure vanilla extract
Optional: up to 1 cup/172 g chocolate, for coating

1. Preheat the oven to 400°F and spread the almonds on a dry half sheet pan (18 by 13 inches). Toast for 5 to 10 minutes, until one shade darker and fragrant. Remove from the oven and set aside.
2. Line a second half sheet pan with parchment paper or a silicone baking mat.
3. Combine the sugar, water, milk, oil, syrup, and salt in a 4-quart pot and stir, being careful not to splash onto the sides of the pot. Bring to a boil. Lower the heat to a simmer. Brush down sides of the pot with a pastry brush dipped in cool water periodically.

4. Meanwhile, grind the almonds into medium-fine pieces by pulsing in a food processor or chopping by hand. Stir the baking soda into the almonds.

5. When the toffee registers 321°F on candy thermometer, immediately remove from the heat. It will jump around a lot, most likely, at this high temperature. Try to stay tough and let it get as darkly caramelized as you can.

6. Whisk in the almond mixture quickly and carefully, then whisk in the vanilla. Stir well.

7. Pour onto the prepared sheet pan. Do not smooth out the toffee with a spatula; just let it be a blob exactly as it came out of the pot (do make some attempt to pour it onto the pan evenly), otherwise it will deflate.

8. Let cool. If desired, temper the chocolate (see page 17) and coat the toffee with a very thin layer of it, then let cool.

9. When cool, break into bite-size pieces. Store in a sealed container in the refrigerator or freezer.

English Toffee Bars

I mean, how do candy bars feel about the gaze? Do they absorb the alienation that results from the split between seeing oneself and seeing oneself through others' eyes and what even about Foucault's concept of panopticism and how, like, capitalism depends it? I'm a pagan non-TERFy ecofeminist transcendentalist, I mean obviously, but those poststructuralists, they really give you something to nosh on you know? And herewith: English Toffee Bars. Intellectual little dudes.

Makes 12 bars

1. Make the Heathen Toffee through step 5 of the previous recipe, but omit the almonds.
2. Then, there are a couple of ways to make these into bars, rather than the amorphous blob they very postmodernly want to be. The easiest is to buy silicone bar molds on the Internet or in your local confectionery supply shop, but what would Foucault have to say about that? Probably lots! Who has the power; how do we use it? Can we DIY toffee bar molds, and in so doing escape the relentless accumulation of capital that defines and inscribes our existence?
3. Yup: pour into a 9-inch square silicone baking pan or metal pan lined on all sides with parchment paper. As soon as your toffee is the slightest bit firm, score it with a knife into two 4½-inch slabs, then each slab crosswise into six 1½ by 4½-inch bar shapes, to make a total of twelve bars. Break along the scoring marks (with the help of a knife or hammer lightly tapped onto a butter knife, if necessary) when it's fully set up. If desired, dip into tempered chocolate.
4. Also? Sometimes I think we will, soon, wrest ourselves free of the overarching power dynamics that seem to so narrowly delineate our innermost selves.

maple honeycomb (sponge toffee)

....

Nothing to do with cereal. If you're English, you know what I mean by "honeycomb." Or if you grew up near Buffalo, New York, you know it as "sponge candy" and you buy it at Wegmans and local candy shops. This is a super simple recipe, one of the easiest in the book. Takes twenty minutes, impresses your candy freak friends. Go for it!

Honeycomb is a superaerated (thanks, baking soda!) toffee that's crispy and light and spongy and lovely. Ours has maple syrup instead of honey and is addictive and maple-toasty and lovely.

Be sure your baking soda is fresh. Mix a cup of warm water and a spoonful of vinegar and stir in a spoonful of baking soda. If it doesn't bubble up, get a fresh box.

As with all toffees, keep your honeycomb in the refrigerator in a tightly sealed container. When you break your big sheet of honeycomb into pieces, you'll have a lot of little crumbs. At our shop, we used to save up these crumbs for my mother, who put them in her coffee, where they melted into sweet maple flavor and finally weaned her off the artificially flavored coffee syrups I relentlessly made fun of her for buying.

Makes 1⅓ pounds toffee

~~~~~~

¼ cup/84 g pure maple syrup (whatever grade you like will work;
    we use a medium dark variety)

½ cup plus 2 tablespoons/170 g Cane Syrup (page 96) or organic corn syrup

2 cups/400 g sugar

¼ cup/45 g water

1½ teaspoons/10 g baking soda

~~~~~~

1. Line a half sheet pan (18 by 13 inches) with a silicone baking mat or parchment paper.
2. Combine all the ingredients, except the baking soda, in a 2- to 4-quart pot. Stir gently until just combined.

3. Heat as high as possible, watching closely, wiping down the sides of the pot with a pastry brush dipped in cold fresh water, until the mixture registers 315°F on a candy thermometer.
4. Turn off the heat, whisk in the baking soda thoroughly (longer and harder than you think you need to, otherwise you'll bite into these weird chunks of it later on), and very quickly pour onto the prepared sheet pan. It will puff up immediately as soon as you stop whisking it. Do not touch, agitate, or smooth out once you've poured it out of the pan (it will deflate). When cool, break into bite-size pieces.
5. We don't scrape our honeycomb pot with a spatula and pour the scrapings onto the honeycomb. The scraped honeycomb toffee is deflated and sad. Instead, pour it into a small pot and gently melt it with a little water to make a different kind of "maple syrup" for pancakes or ice cream.

matzo toffee

· ·

Oh gosh, I'm just excited for ya. This recipe is so great! And simple. The only tricks to it are to drizzle the chocolate in very thin lines, so you don't get clumps of it that take over the flavor of the toffee, and to sprinkle the sea salt from high above the pan, so it evenly disperses and no one gets a big salt bite.

Unlike with every other temperature-dependent recipe in this book, don't stress about stopping the caramel when it gets to the correct temperature. Because you're going to bake the toffee anyway, the temperature isn't as important for the final texture of your confection.

Makes a little less than 1 pound toffee

5 (7 by 7-inch) sheets matzo

1½ cups packed/325 g light brown sugar

¾ cup/220 g coconut milk

½ teaspoon/3 g sea salt

¼ pound chocolate, for drizzling

Fleur de sel sea salt, for sprinkling

1. Preheat the oven to 350° F.
2. Line a half sheet pan (18 by 13 inches) with parchment paper or silicone baking sheets. Set the matzo on the lined pan in an even layer, breaking it when necessary to make it fit evenly.
3. Place the milk, brown sugar, and sea salt (not fleur de sel) in a 2- to 4-quart pot and heat over medium heat. Cook until the mixture registers 225°F on a candy thermometer. Remove from the heat.
4. Using tongs, dip the sheets of matzo into the toffee until covered, letting it drip off a bit, then transfer back to their places on the prepared pan. Pour any leftover toffee evenly onto the matzo.
5. Bake for 15 minutes, watching to make sure it doesn't burn. If it looks like it is starting to burn, lower the oven temperature to 325°F.

6. After 15 to 25 minutes (depending on your oven), the toffee should have bubbled up and turned a rich golden brown. Remove from the oven. We press our Matzo Toffee between parchment sheets and sheet pans at this point, to ensure nice flat sheets, but if you don't mind somewhat wavy sheets of toffee, don't worry about it.

7. When cool, temper the chocolate (see page 17; you'll have leftover chocolate, but tempering less than half a pound is annoying) and drizzle it over the Matzo Toffee. While the chocolate is wet, sprinkle it with the fleur de sel.

8. Let cool completely, then break into pieces and store in an airtight container in the refrigerator.

peanut butter toffee bars

· ·

We make a lot of peanut butter confections. We're American, and Americans like peanut butter, and we're mostly all vegans, and vegans also like peanut butter. Also, peanut butter is a naturally vegan fat that plays well in confectionery recipes. We've had to drop this bar from our regular lineup, though, because it's ludicrous to make it on a large scale. For a long time when you went to our website to buy it, we just listed the recipe instead of an option to buy it. More than one of our customers made it out of sheer desperation at not being able to buy it (an intern once wooed us by bringing them to an interview), and now you can, too.

This recipe is unlike any others in this book. It's the only dry caramel in the book (just melted sugar, cooked to a high temperature, and stirred constantly, unlike all other caramels that are stirred as minimally as possible), and it uses a technique called leaf croquant that basically entails making a croissantlike layered dough from a hot sugar mass. It's all extremely exciting. What you end up with is a crispy, flaky, crunchy bar that tastes similar to and much better than a certain supermarket peanut buttery candy bar.

Once you've gotten the hang of it and get obsessed with this bar, which you will and which you will, the recipe scales up perfectly.

Be sure you have all your tools and ingredients ready before you start—this one goes fast.

Makes 12 bars

Filling

½ cup plus 2 tablespoons/150 g all-natural smooth peanut butter

¼ cup/23 g confectioners' sugar

1 tablespoon/11 g Cane Syrup (page 96) or organic corn syrup

Caramel

¼ teaspoon/2 g freshly squeezed lemon juice

¾ cup/168 g granulated sugar

2 tablespoons/22 g Cane Syrup (page 96) or organic corn syrup

1. Line two half sheet pans (18 by 13 inches) with silicone baking mats or parchment paper.
2. Prepare the filling: Melt the peanut butter in a double boiler or in a microwave. (If it's warm out, just let it sit out an hour or so.) Sift in the confectioners' sugar, add the syrup, and knead until malleable and smooth with a spatula or your hands.
3. Using a bench scraper or offset spatula, form the peanut butter dough into a 7-inch square on one of the lined pans. Keep warm in an oven set to its lowest temperature.
4. Prepare the caramel: Coat the bottom of a 2-quart pot with the lemon juice, then add the granulated sugar and make a dry caramel by cooking over high heat, stirring constantly, until the sugar is evenly melted, not grainy at all, and becomes a golden amber color. It's important to ensure the caramel is perfectly smooth with no unmelted sugar. This will take at least 10 minutes.
5. Lower the heat to medium, add the syrup, and stir until emulsified. The caramel should be smooth, not lumpy, and a beautiful amber color.
6. Pour the caramel into a rough 9-inch square onto the second sheet pan. The caramel will cool very quickly. As it cools, use a bench scraper to form it into a square. Use a spatula to scrape the caramel off the bench scraper and back onto the square of caramel.
7. Place the square of filling on the caramel square, leaving about 1 inch caramel-free on all sides. Use the bench scraper to pat it into a good, tidy square. The tidier you are during these initial steps, the more you'll appreciate it later.
8. Fold the mat or parchment and caramel over the filling to enclose it in thirds, like a fat letter. Peel off mat and tightly seal edges of the caramel to envelop the filling.
9. As you're working, you'll want to periodically return the entire candy slab to the low oven to warm it to a workable consistency. Watch it carefully and don't let it melt so much that you lose its shape, but don't hesitate to warm it enough that it's completely pliable. Now might be a time to remind you about that "practice makes perfect" thing.
10. When the slab is pliable again, roll out the slab into a thin rectangle, then fold into thirds. Repeat this process three more times, to make four "turns" total. Don't overmix the dough, or you'll lose flakiness.
11. After the final turn, roll the slab into a ¼-inch-thick 9-inch square. Cut in half into two 4½-inch slabs, then cut each slab crosswise into six 1½ by 4½-inch bars, to make a total of twelve bars. Store in a tightly sealed container in the refrigerator for up to six weeks.

CANDY BARS

I was giving this talk at NYU to smart business students (i.e., Future Capitalists) about being a so-called anarchist business owner who started her business with no capital, who sort of didn't even know what *capital* meant, and at one point I was talking about how high prices have to be to pay real costs all down the line, to chocolatiers and farmworkers and eco-packaging printing companies and the whole tortured Apocalypse Now supply chain, and I said, "I mean, okay, I don't know what a Snickers bar costs these days, but I know my candy bars cost a lot more—and the entire class yelled out ONE DOLLAR. And I was just like,

ONE DOLLAR?

We sell these for between nine and twelve. They're worth it! But you can bring those costs down a little by making them yourself. For one thing, you don't need to package them. For another, you're probably not going to pay yourself to make them.

So, you've made some caramel- and some ganache-based confections. You're well on your way to becoming a bona fide candywitch. Let's put your sugar skills together and make some candy bars. If you've made a recipe or two from each section (or even if you haven't), these recipes are just combining them into slabs, cutting the slabs into bar form, and dipping them in chocolate. These are amazing and are going to blow the mind of anyone who tastes them. A steal at twice the price, but boy, everyone would be mad.

bourbon caramel chile fudge bars

Fudgy as the day is long, this wild baby showcases your favorite bourbon. We developed this bar in partnership with our local distillery, Tuthilltown Spirits, to spotlight its Hudson Four Grain Bourbon. It's impossible to exaggerate how incredibly boozy this bar is. A lot of spice cuts all that whiskey wildness. This bar is incredibly easy to make. Like the fudge layer in the Earl Grey bar (page 199), it's basically a caramel with chocolate added at the end, as if it was a ganache. Be sure to stir in the chocolate thoroughly, for a perfect texture.

Makes 12 bars

¾ cup plus 1 tablespoon/200 g coconut milk

1¾ cups/300 g brown sugar

1 cup/200 g sugar

½ cup/150 g Cane Syrup (page 96) or organic corn syrup

1 teaspoon/5 g fleur de sel sea salt

½ cup plus 3 tablespoons/125 g bourbon, plus ⅓ cup/70 g

1½ tablespoons/8 g chipotle chile powder

1 tablespoon/7 g ancho chile powder

1 teaspoon/5 g cream of tartar

1½ teaspoons/7 g pure vanilla extract

1¾ cups/½ pound chopped dark chocolate, for dipping (optional)

1. Set out a 9-inch square silicone pan. If not made of silicone or other nonstick material, line it on all sides with parchment paper.
2. Combine the milk, brown sugar, sugar, syrup, salt, and ½ cup plus 3 tablespoons/125 g of the bourbon in a 2- to 4-quart pot. Stir gently, then bring to a boil over medium heat without stirring. While the mixture is cooking, wash down the sides of the pan with a pastry brush dipped in

cool water every 10 minutes or so, to prevent sugar crystals from forming on the side of the pot, jumping into the caramel, and making it gritty.

3. Cook over medium-low heat (the mixture should be simmering, but not climbing the sides of the pan) until the caramel registers 250°F on a candy thermometer. Stir in the chipotle and ancho chile powders.

4. Continue to cook until the caramel reaches 270°F on a candy thermometer.

5. Turn off the heat and carefully stir in the remaining ⅓ cup/70 g of bourbon, cream of tartar, vanilla, and chocolate with a whisk.

6. Pour the caramel into the prepared pan. Let sit at room temperature or in the refrigerator until cool and set, about an hour. Turn out onto a sheet pan lined with parchment (don't worry about lining the sides), then use a serrated knife frequently dipped into hot water (a tall, conical container is best to hold it, such as a 4-cup liquid measuring cup or flower vase) and dried with a clean kitchen towel to cut the square into two 4½-inch slabs, then cut each slab crosswise into six 1½ by 4½-inch bars, to make a total of twelve bars.

7. Eat as is (store in the refrigerator so bars don't lose their shape) or temper the chocolate (page 17), and dip the bars in it, using a dipping fork, regular fork, or your fingers.

8. Store the dipped bars in a tightly sealed container at room temperature, where they will keep for up to 6 weeks, or in the refrigerator, where they will keep 2 months.

earl grey and Preserved orange bars

Adrienne worked on this one. You will never meet a vegan more intense about veganism than Adrienne. Not in an annoying way. Adrienne is way, way too introverted and quiet to be annoying. She just has her beliefs and is steadfast about them. Unlike Maresa and me, Adrienne would never wear thrifted wool sweaters. Adrienne's veganism is strict and simple: no animal products. It's not that easy, out in the real world, but Adrienne doesn't live in the real world, and I like this about her.

Adrienne's life is devoted to her pets, a constant stream of rescued lab rats who are (1) adorable and (2) constantly dying and in need of expensive medical care. The tiny nebulizers and pricey medications, the special vet an hour away: Adrienne lives the philosophy of true animal rights, a belief that even the smallest beings are deserving of a good life.

Work-wise, Adrienne's famously never made a mistake, is fastidious about profit margins, regularly finds ways to bump up our sales while not compromising our ethics.

After about four years of working alongside Adrienne, I said to her, "Okay, here's my theory. Let me know if I'm right. You totally and completely see how screwed the world is. Your politics are somewhere to the left of Noam Chomsky, whom you've never read because he's a man. The world is completely disgusting to you on most levels. Instead of working as a traditional activist to change it, you figure that you'll do your part by living apart from it, giving a good life to some creatures who depend on you, and interacting as little as possible with the horrors of the patriarchal, meat-eating, capitalist society you despise." She didn't pause from the caramel she was spreading, just quietly breathed, "Yeah, sure. Okay."

Adrienne, this strange and wonderful and quiet and very tall person you'll probably never meet because she wouldn't like you, helped bring this bar into existence and I'm so grateful.

But. This bar is so fantastic. Bergamot (extra-good bitter-perfume-lemony citrus o' yr dreams) plus black tea in a fudgy ganachey thing plus caramel cram-jammed with preserved orange. We garnish these with dried calendula petals from our shop garden; you can sprinkle anything you'd like on it, including nothing.

To make the preserved orange called for, see the Preserved Lemons recipe (page 149) and use oranges instead. If you don't want to wait for your oranges to preserve, use an equivalent amount of chopped fresh oranges, for a differently lovely flavor. Make an effort to seek out pure culinary-grade orange oil (not orange extract or essential oil) for this recipe; it's the key to the great citrus flavor.

Makes 16 bars

Preserved orange caramel

1 cup/240 g coconut milk

¼ cup/42 g coconut oil

1¾ cups/375 g sugar

½ cup/150 g Cane Syrup (page 96) or organic corn syrup

1 tablespoon/8 g fleur de sel sea salt

1 vanilla bean, split and scraped

2 tablespoons/15 g ground preserved orange peel and flesh
   (roughly ½ peel and ½ flesh, don't be too fussy about it; see page 149)

1 teaspoon/5 g cream of tartar

1½ teaspoons/7 g pure vanilla extract

½ teaspoon/3 g culinary-grade orange oil (see headnote)

1. Set out a 9-inch square silicone pan. If not made of silicone or other nonstick material, line it on all sides with parchment paper.
2. Combine the milk, oil, sugar, syrup, and salt in a 2- to 4-quart pot. Stir gently, then bring to a boil over medium heat without stirring. While the mixture is cooking, wash down the sides of the pan with a pastry brush dipped in cool water every 10 minutes or so, to prevent sugar crystals from forming on the side of the pot, jumping into the caramel, and making it gritty.
3. Cook over medium-low heat (the mixture should be simmering, but not climbing the sides of the pan) until the caramel registers 261°F on a candy thermometer.
4. Turn off the heat and stir in the remaining ingredients with a whisk.
5. Pour the caramel into the prepared pan. Let sit in the refrigerator until cool and set, about an hour.

Earl Grey fudge layer

1 scant cup/220 g coconut milk

2 tablespoons/11 g, plus 2 teaspoons/6 g Earl Grey tea leaves

¼ cup/42 g coconut oil

1½ cups/300 g sugar

½ cup/145 g Cane Syrup (page 96) or organic corn syrup

2 teaspoons/12 g sea salt

1 teaspoon/5 g pure vanilla extract

1 teaspoon/5 g cream of tartar

½ cup plus 2 tablespoons/100 g chopped bittersweet chocolate, for dipping

1. Bring the milk to a boil in a small pot and remove from the heat. Add the 2 tablespoons/11 g of the Earl Grey tea and steep for 5 minutes. Strain out and discard the tea leaves.
2. Combine the milk mixture, oil, sugar, syrup, and salt in a 2- to 4-quart pot. Stir gently, then bring to a boil over medium heat without stirring. While the mixture is cooking, wash down the sides of the pan with a pastry brush dipped in cool water every 10 minutes or so, to prevent sugar crystals from forming on the side of the pot, jumping into the caramel, and making it gritty.
3. When the caramel comes to 259°F, remove from the heat and whisk in the vanilla, cream of tartar, and the remaining 2 teaspoons/6 g of Earl Grey tea leaves.
4. Pour over the cooled orange caramel. Let sit for 1 hour at room temperature to firm up.
5. Turn out onto a sheet pan lined with parchment, then use a serrated knife frequently dipped into hot water (a tall, conical container is best to hold it, such as a 4-cup liquid measuring cup or flower vase) and dried with a clean kitchen towel to cut the square to make two 4½-inch slabs, then each slab crosswise into eight 1⅛ by 4½-inch bars, to make a total of sixteen bars.
6. Keep the cut bars in a tightly closed container in the freezer so they keep their shape. Temper the chocolate (see page 17), and dip the bars into it, using a dipping fork, regular fork, or your fingers.
7. Store the dipped bars in a tightly sealed container at room temperature, where they will keep for up to 6 weeks, or in the refrigerator, where they will keep for 2 months.

(recipe photo shown on page 200)

hazelnut sugar plum caramel bars

···

This bar is a Christmas bar, invented by this Jew in December to be eaten in December to give you Christmas Feelings™. We all love it so much that we typically make it about ten months out of the year. We do what we want!!

Our gianduja (a hazelnut spread like Nutella—say "jian-doo-ya") is intense and ultrarich, vegan (surprise!), much less sugary, much more hazelnut-forward, and much more concentrated than commercial varieties.

It's also good to make this bar when you can get fat sun-warmed plums from your local farmers' market. We use Italian prune plums from Wright's Farm down the road because they're intense and not watery, but any nice purple plum will work. A green or yellow plum, such as a greengage or shiro, will make a brighter, tarter caramel, differently good, not quite as Christmassy.

Puree the plums and strain them, pressing out as much water as you can, to make the plum puree needed for the recipe.

On the one hand, this is a recipe made up of literally five other recipes. On the other hand, each of these recipes teaches you a fundamental and useful confectionery skill and is a gem of a preparation that can be eaten alone. Taken together, this powerhouse bar is not only one of the best recipes in this book, it's just one of the best things you'll ever put in your mouth ever. Pros and cons, you know?

Makes 16 bars

Salted sugar plum caramel

1¼ cups/312 g coconut milk

⅓ cup/56 g coconut oil

2¾ cups/533 g sugar

7 tablespoons/174 g Cane Syrup (page 96) or organic corn syrup

¾ teaspoon/2 g fleur de sel sea salt

¾ cup/200 g plum puree

¾ tablespoon/7 g Snowy Christmas Morning Spice Mix (recipe follows)

1 teaspoon/5 g cream of tartar

1. Set out a 9-inch silicone pan.
2. Combine the milk, oil, sugar, syrup, and salt in a 2- to 4-quart pot. Stir gently, then bring to a boil over medium heat without stirring. While the mixture is cooking, wash down the sides of the pan with a pastry brush dipped in cool water every 10 minutes or so, to prevent sugar crystals from forming on the side of the pot, jumping into the caramel, and making it gritty.
3. Cook over medium-low heat (the mixture should be simmering, but not climbing the sides of the pan) until the caramel registers approximately 250°F on a candy thermometer.
4. Add the plum puree and spice mix. Gently stir the bottom of the pot a few times to make sure the mixture isn't burning.
5. Continue to cook until the mixture reaches 261°F on thermometer.
6. Remove the pan from the heat and stir in the cream of tartar.
7. Pour the caramel into the prepared pan. Let cool in the refrigerator until cool and set, about an hour.

Gianduja meltaway

1¼ cups/495 g gianduja (recipe follows), gently warmed in double boiler or microwave if not just made and fairly fluid

1½ cups/225 g ganache (page 25), gently warmed in double boiler or microwave if not just made and fairly fluid

½ teaspoon/2 g fleur de sel sea salt

2 cups/262 g hazelnut praline (recipe follows)

1. Ensure the gianduja and ganache are roughly the same temperature and fluidity level before combining them.
2. Combine the gianduja with the ganache, salt, and praline in a large bowl.

To assemble

Fleur de sel sea salt

1 pound chocolate, for dipping

1. Sprinkle a pinch or two of salt over the plum caramel in the pan.

2. Spread the gianduja meltaway over the caramel. Let sit at room temperature for 1 hour to firm up.

3. Turn out onto a sheet pan lined with parchment, then use a serrated knife frequently dipped into hot water (a tall, conical container is best to hold it, such as a 4-cup liquid measuring cup or flower vase) and dried with a clean kitchen towel to cut the square into two 4½-inch slabs, then cut each slab crosswise into eight 1⅛ by 4½-inch bars, to make a total of sixteen bars.

4. Keep the cut bars in a tightly closed container in the freezer so they keep their shape. Temper the chocolate (see page 17), and dip the bars into it, using a dipping fork, regular fork, or your fingers.

5. Store the dipped bars in a tightly sealed container at room temperature, where they will keep for up to 6 weeks, or in the refrigerator, where they will keep for 2 months.

Snowy Christmas Morning Spice Mix

This spice mix makes more than you need for the recipe, but if you're going to go to the trouble of grinding spices, why not make a good amount? Unlike sticky-sweet Christmassy spice blends, this one is austere and old-fashioned, in the vein of truly spicy gingerbread and other darkly fragrant Christmas sweets. Stir it into hot chocolate, steamed milk, or coffee, or sprinkle it on pancakes or oatmeal or chocolate chip cookies before you bake them.

Urfa pepper is a supertasty smoky, chocolatey, sour, not-too-spicy pepper, but if you can't find it use smoked sweet paprika; Aleppo, chipotle, or ancho chile powder; or, in a real pinch, regular chili powder.

Makes 3 tablespoons spice mix

2 tablespoons/10 g whole star anise

1 tablespoon/5 g whole black peppercorns (even better: long pepper)

1½ teaspoons/4 g whole urfa pepper

1. Grind all the spices together until finely ground.

Gianduja

If you use chocolate that is melted just enough to be fluid but not technically tempered, your gianduja will be just fine. Gianduja keeps for two months in the refrigerator, longer in the freezer. This recipe makes more than you need, but it's delicious and you will be happy to have extra.

Makes 6 cups gianduja

4 cups/500 g hazelnuts
3¼ cups/500 g confectioners' sugar
2 cups/500 g tempered chocolate (see page 17)

1. In a 350°F oven, toast the hazelnuts on a dry sheet pan until fragrant and one shade darker, 5 to 10 minutes. Remove from the oven and let cool. When cool enough to handle, lightly rub to remove the skins. This is optional and doesn't make a huge difference in the gianduja, but I always do it because I really enjoy rolling hot hazelnuts around in my perpetually cold hands, and I'm convinced it makes more of a difference than it does.
2. Liquefy the hazelnuts with a few tablespoons of the sugar in a food processor. Process until as smooth as possible.
3. Add the remaining sugar and tempered chocolate and mix until emulsified.
4. Store in a container in the refrigerator.

Hazelnut Praline

This recipe makes about double what you need for this bar, because **you are going to snack on this. A lot.** It's also a fun, easy, quick recipe you can't really screw up. Praline is intentionally crystallized caramel! No washing down of pots here—a creamy-crunchy consistency is what you're going for, so instead of never stirring like when making caramel candies, you stir constantly.

Makes 3½ cups

¾ cup plus 2 tablespoons/175 g granulated sugar
¾ cup plus 2 tablespoons/175 g light brown sugar
6 tablespoons/140 g coconut milk

3 tablespoons/35 g coconut oil

1½ cups/175 g hazelnuts, toasted and chopped coarsely

½ teaspoon/2 g sea salt

½ teaspoon/2 g pure vanilla extract

1. Line a half sheet pan (18 by 13 inches) with parchment paper or a silicone baking mat.
2. Combine the sugars, milk, and oil in a 2- to 4-quart pot over medium heat. Stir constantly until the mixture comes to 230°F, then add the nuts and salt and cook to 237°F while continuing to stir.
3. Remove from the heat. Allow to cool, undisturbed, to 212°F. Add the vanilla.
4. Using a wooden spoon, stir vigorously until the mixture begins to look creamy, a minute or so.
5. Pour out onto the prepared sheet pan. When cool, break or chop into bite-size pieces. Store in a tightly sealed container in the refrigerator for up to 6 weeks.

Tahini Meltaways (page 226)

fruit, vegetable, and creamy confections. plus a cookie

alfajores

· ·

Vegans, by necessity, are expert ingredient swappers. This has led to ingenious inventions, but it has also led to a game of Telephone where omnivorous dishes become less and less of themselves the deeper into the vegan world they tread. Everyone who was vegan in the 1990s or 2000s has had lasagne with crumbled tofu seasoned with nutritional yeast and salt masquerading as down-at-heels ricotta. It's something, but it's not lasagne in the deepest meaning of the word.

And so it is with dulce de leche. Processed vegan margarine waved over the stove with some sugar does not a dulce de leche make, no matter how many blogs might try to convince us it's so. Dates + soy milk—no.

I wanted to make the real thing; that is, I wanted to do what pretty much the entire world does when they make dulce de leche: boil a can of sweetened condensed milk and open it to magically reveal a thick, spoonable confection, something with structure and heft and a sense of self-worth. *Dulce de leche* means "milk jam" and that jammy, intense texture was what I was looking for.

I knew boiling a can of coconut milk wouldn't yield anything like what I was looking for, and while I could make a workable sauce from coconut milk and brown sugar cooked for a few hours on the stovetop, it didn't have the body of true canned dulce de leche.

When sweetened condensed coconut milk, now available in most health food stores, came on the market, I nabbed a few cans and went to work.

Boiled in hot water, what emerges is something with a sense of self, something with integrity and the deep richness that can only come from long exposure to the beautifully indirect heat of a hot water bath while sealed in the airless sugary milky world of an aluminum can. Dulce de leche, which even the nonvegans I fed it to proclaimed authentic and supremely not coconutty. I indulged in a quick feeling of glee at being alive when such magical new vegan products were being brought to market, then got to work making alfajores, the traditional Latin American shortbread cookie.

Makes 24 sandwich cookies

½ cup/100 g sugar

½ cup/84 g coconut oil, at room temperature

¼ cup/50 g olive oil

1 tablespoon/10 g brandy, Kahlúa, or whiskey

Zest of 1 lemon

2 teaspoons/10 g pure vanilla extract

5 tablespoons/60 g coconut milk

1¼ cups/156 g all-purpose flour, plus more for dusting

¾ cup/100 g cornstarch or potato starch

¼ teaspoon/1 g baking soda

1 teaspoon/5 g baking powder

¾ teaspoon/5 g sea salt

1 recipe dulce de leche (recipe follows)

1 pound chocolate, for dipping (optional)

1. In the bowl of a stand mixer fitted with the paddle attachment, beat the sugar, coconut oil, and olive oil together until fully incorporated and fluffy.
2. Add the brandy, lemon zest, vanilla, and milk and mix to combine.
3. Combine the remaining ingredients, except the dulce de leche and chocolate, in a separate bowl, then add to the mixer bowl and mix just to combine. The dough will seem very wet. For now, do not add more flour.
4. Cover the mixer bowl with plastic wrap and chill the dough until firm, an hour or more.
5. Line two half sheet pans (18 by 13 inches) with parchment paper.
6. On a lightly floured surface, roll out the dough to ⅛-inch thickness. If the dough is still very wet, sparingly add a little more flour at a time. Use a 2-inch round cutter or drinking glass to cut out cookies and place on the prepared sheet pans. Reroll the scraps to use all the dough. Refrigerate for 30 minutes, or until firm.
7. Meanwhile, preheat the oven to 350°F.
8. Bake for 6 to 8 minutes, or until the cookies just start to turn golden brown.
9. Remove from the oven and transfer the cookies to a rack to cool.
10. Turn half of the cookies upside down and pipe dulce de leche filling generously onto the overturned cookies. Top each with one of the remaining cookies. If the dulce de leche becomes too liquidy, refrigerate or freeze until firm enough to pipe.
11. If desired, dip each cookie into melted tempered chocolate (see page 17).

Dulce de Leche

~~~~~~

2 (7.4-ounce) cans sweetened condensed coconut milk

~~~~~~

1. Remove the labels from the cans. Put the cans on their side in a 4-quart pot and cover with 4 inches of water. Bring to a boil over medium heat, then lower the heat to a simmer and cook for 4 hours, turning the cans (but still leaving on their side) once in a while to make sure they are evenly cooked.
2. Remove from the heat, let cans cool down, remove from the pot with tongs, and carefully open. Whisk or stir to combine the dulce de leche thoroughly.
3. Transfer the dulce de leche into a piping bag or sandwich bag with a corner snipped off. Refrigerate until firm and pipable, 30 minutes to 1 hour.
4. Unopened cans of dulce de leche can be stored at room temperature for months, and opened cans can be stored in the refrigerator in a container for a month.

alexis's coconut chews

. . . .

There's nothing Alexis isn't good at, from cooking to penmanship to managing people to artfully layering various shades of sand, tan, beige, and ecru-colored clothing on her body. Six years ago, Kate went to her college thesis show, full of gorgeous ceramics and a whip-smart design sensibility already fully formed, and the next week, she happened to apply to work at the shop. Now she's the reason we ask in job interviews whether people consider themselves artists: in time, we've come to realize that that one question, more than anything else, is a predictor of what kind of chocolatier you'll be. We can teach pastry skills, we can teach how to work in a commercial kitchen, but if you don't consider yourself an artist it's going to be rough.

As a special bonus, Alexis is the rare nonvegan in our world, so when we want to rip off nonvegan sweets, she can go eat them and tell us how close we are.

This stylish bonbon is just like Alexis, who developed it: its strength is in its simplicity, with no wasted motion or flavorings. If you want to make it wilder, try this curry variation: add 7 to 8 teaspoons, to taste, sweet (or hot!) curry powder to the coconut while it's toasting.

Makes 48 chews

3¾ cups/324 g unsweetened coconut flakes

1 cup/240 g coconut milk

½ cup/78 g confectioners' sugar

½ teaspoon/2 g cornstarch

¼ cup/42 g coconut oil

1 teaspoon/7 g pure vanilla extract

1 teaspoon/7 g coconut extract

⅓ cup/125 g Cane Syrup (page 96) or organic corn syrup

¼ teaspoon/2 g sea salt

1 pound chocolate, for dipping (optional)

1. Toast the coconut in a dry skillet over low heat or in a low oven, stirring often, until it turns light brown, about 10 minutes. Transfer half of the toasted coconut to a large heatproof bowl, reserving the remaining coconut separately.
2. Combine the milk, confectioners' sugar, cornstarch, and oil in a 4-quart pot and bring to a boil, and boil until it begins to thicken.
3. Pour the warm milk mixture into the bowl of toasted coconut and combine.
4. Process the remaining toasted coconut flakes in a food processor for 30 seconds, or until fairly broken down. Add the wet coconut mixture and the remaining ingredients, except the chocolate, and process until a paste forms. Don't worry about getting it smooth; you just want a nice cohesive paste, not a puree.
5. Spread the paste as evenly as possible in a 9-inch square silicone pan, pressing the mixture down firmly.
6. Refrigerate until firm, then cut into eight 1-inch strips, and then cut each strip crosswise into six 1½-inch pieces, to make four dozen rectangles.
7. Eat as is, or dip each square into tempered chocolate (see page 17).
8. Store the dipped bars in a tightly sealed container at room temperature, where they will keep for up to 6 weeks, or in the refrigerator, where they will keep for 2 months.

latke bonbons

In the vernacular of chocolate-covered potato chips, yet more Jewish, I present the Latke Bonbon. I'm so pleased with this little treat. It's simple and pretty much perfect. A plate of these at a Hanukkah party is wildly impressive.

This latke is the one I make for my friends every Hanukkah, just with half as much onion. Double the onion and add some applesauce and vegan sour cream, and you're ready for dinner. There's no egg replacer in this recipe—the potato starch in the grated potatoes binds everything nicely, so be sure not to squeeze it all out or you'll be left with dry burnt potato shreds instead of nicely fried latkes.

You'll need a pastry bag fitted with the smallest plain (not fluted or scalloped) tip you can find, or a disposable pastry bag or resealable plastic bag (cut a tip to be about the size of a thick pencil lead) for this. If you're good at making cornets, the little parchment paper cones, by all means make a cornet, but if you're good at cornets, you don't need to be told to make one, I'm guessing.

Makes 40 bonbons

Potato latkes

¼ yellow onion, roughly 3½ ounces/100 g

4 large russet potatoes (1½ pounds), peeled

1½ teaspoons/8 g sea salt

A few twists of freshly ground black pepper

1 teaspoon/5 g baking powder

¼ cup/35 g matzo meal (buy it or grind up matzo crackers until superfine)

Olive oil, for parchment

1. Preheat the oven to 375°F with a half sheet pan (18 by 13 inches) in it.
2. Grate the onion and potatoes on the large holes of a box grater or with the shredding disk of a food processor (the onion can also be minced). Don't squeeze the water out of the potatoes.
3. Combine the grated onion and potatoes, salt, pepper, baking powder, and matzo meal in a large bowl. Toss until evenly mixed.
4. Line the heated sheet pan with parchment paper and spread a thin layer of olive oil on the parchment. Spread the matzo mixture on the prepared sheet pan and bake until deeply golden brown. To ensure a good flavor that won't be overpowered by chocolate, bake the latke mixture until it's a darker color than you would want for latkes ordinarily. Rotate the pan frequently and, if possible, pick up the entire sheet of latke mixture and flip it. Continue to bake on the other side until deep golden brown and rather dried out–looking. Remove from the oven and let cool.

To assemble

~~~~~~~~~~~~~~~~~~~~~~~

1 pound dark chocolate

Fleur de sel sea salt

~~~~~~~~~~~~~~~~~~~~~~~

1. In a food processor, pulse the latke sheet until ground into a fine powder. If your latkes weren't baked long enough and your mixture becomes a paste, you can dehydrate it for a few hours at 110°F, or dry it out in an oven set to the lowest temperature. Measure out 1 cup plus 2 table-spoons/166 g of the latke powder to use for the bonbons.
2. Temper the chocolate (see 17).
3. Using an offset spatula, spread twelve circles of chocolate onto a parchment sheet, each about 2 inches across. Don't stress about the size so much.
4. Working quickly, using a looping motion, cover the chocolate circles with loose loops of chocolate. While the chocolate is still wet, sprinkle one circle with a layer (roughly 1 teaspoon) of latke powder, then a sprinkle of the salt. Continue with remaining eleven circles. Aim for flat pancake-looking bonbons, not pyramids.
5. Whenever your chocolate starts hardening, warm it a little with a hair dryer. If it hardens up too much, very gently remelt it, so it stays in temper.
6. Pipe each bonbon with another layer of chocolate loops and sprinkle with another layer of latke powder, then another layer of salt.
7. Pipe with another layer of chocolate and finish with a light sprinkle of salt.

potato chip bonbons

. . . .

Basically, I'm just excited for you. Homemade potato chips softly set into silky fudgy ganache—it's simple and perfect.

   If you don't want to make homemade potato chips, you have absolute permission to buy the junkiest/tastiest ones you can find and use those instead. Standard baking potatoes are perfect for chips, though any potato will work. Fresher potatoes make a lighter, tastier chip. You can skip the vinegar soaking step, but it makes crispier chips, which are important to guard against softening when they're mixed with the other ingredients. This recipe makes a lot of potato chips. You can halve it if you don't like potato chips. Some of the potato-infused coconut oil you're left with after frying is used in the bonbon. You can use the remaining oil for other frying projects, adding another layer of flavor to sautéed vegetables, or slathering all over yourself for a potato-scented emollient experience.

Makes 45 bonbons

1½ cups/120 g potato chips, plus more for garnishing (recipe follows)

1 cup/162 g dark brown sugar

½ cup/150 g Cane Syrup (page 96) or organic corn syrup

¾ cup/180 g coconut milk

¼ cup/42 g potato chip frying oil or coconut oil

2 teaspoons/18 g red miso

½ teaspoon/5 g sea salt

¾ cup/130 g dark chocolate

1 teaspoon/5 g smoked salt

1 pound chocolate, for dipping

Garnish: small potato chip pieces

1. Grind the potato chips to a fine powder (not a paste) in a food processor or spice grinder. Weigh out ½ cup/40 g and set aside.
2. Combine the brown sugar, syrup, milk, oil, miso, and sea salt in a 4-quart pot. Stir gently, then bring to a boil over medium heat without stirring. While the mixture is cooking, wash down the

sides of the pan with a pastry brush dipped in cool water every 10 minutes or so, to prevent sugar crystals from forming on the side of the pot, jumping into the caramel, and making it gritty.

3. Cook over medium-low heat (the mixture should be simmering, but not climbing the sides of the pan) until the caramel registers 240°F on a candy thermometer.

4. Remove from the heat and whisk in the dark chocolate, smoked salt, and 1 cup/80 g of the ground potato chips. Whisk until emulsified.

5. Pour the mixture into a 9-inch square silicone pan. Sprinkle reserved ½ cup/40 g of ground potato chips over the top.

6. Refrigerate, covered with plastic wrap, until cooled and set, about an hour. Turn out onto another sheet pan lined with parchment (don't worry about lining the sides), then use a serrated knife frequently dipped into hot water (a tall, conical container is best to hold it, such as a 4-cup liquid measuring cup or flower vase) and dried with a clean kitchen towel to cut the square crosswise into nine 1-inch rows and then each row crosswise into 5 pieces, to make into 45 pieces.

7. Temper the dipping chocolate (see page 17), and dip the bonbons into it, using a dipping fork, regular fork, or your fingers. Garnish with a small potato chip piece while the chocolate is wet.

8. The bonbons should be eaten within 3 weeks for maximum crispy freshness, but will keep for 1 month in a tightly sealed container in the refrigerator.

Potato Chips

Makes 6 cups

2 pounds baking potatoes, unpeeled
10 tablespoons/130 g apple cider vinegar or white wine vinegar
6 cups/760 g coconut oil
Sea salt

1. Slice the potatoes as thinly as possible (about ⅛ inch) using a mandoline, slicing disk on a food processor, Y-shaped vegetable peeler, or a good sharp knife and confidence.

2. Rinse the potatoes in several changes of cold water.

3. Dilute the vinegar with 8 cups water in a plastic or ceramic bowl (metal can make the chips taste metallic) and soak the chips for 1 hour. Drain and pat thoroughly dry.

4. Heat the oil to 300°F in a 4-quart pot. Fry the potatoes in small batches, being sure not to crowd the pan, for 4 to 5 minutes, or until the oil stops bubbling completely, poking them a lot with a slotted spoon or wire skimmer (also known as a spider) to make sure they're not sticking together. The potatoes should be a little less browned than you'd like them to be, a medium golden brown, when you lift them out of the oil, because they will continue to darken a little. Be sure the oil comes back to 300°F before adding a new batch of potatoes.
5. Drain on paper towels and sprinkle with sea salt.
6. Store in an airtight container at room temperature.

rock scramble

. . . .

A tumble of hippie cornflakes, pistachios, vegan mini marshmallows, and good sea salt softly swaddled in a dark chocolate cloak, this is my attempt to make a stoner sweet in the GORPesque trail mixy vernacular that isn't as fussy or precious as most of our confections. We use glorious salted pistachios from California, but any shelled (do you ever think about how *shelled* and *unshelled* mean the same thing? Or that you only drive on a parkway and only park on a driveway?) pistachios will do—don't get those weird red dyed ones!

Rock Scramble is named for what you do when you're hanging out in our heart-home, the Shawangunk Ridge, which lures climbers and hikers from all over the world.

Makes 1 pound scramble

6 ounces/170 g (½ box) all-natural frosted flakes–type cereal
 (we use Envirokids Lightly Frosted Amazon Flakes)
6 ounces/170 g vegan mini marshmallows
3 ounces/85 g whole, shelled pistachios
½ pound/145 g dark chocolate
Fleur de sel sea salt

1. Mix the cereal, marshmallows, and nuts together in a large, heatproof bowl.
2. Barely melt the chocolate in a double boiler or microwave until just liquid. Mix the melted chocolate into the cereal mixture. You can also temper the chocolate for this recipe (see page 17), but if you just gently melt it, it most likely won't fall out of temper and will be fine.
3. Sprinkle with sea salt to taste.
4. Break up into small clusters and package into bags, eat, etc.
5. Store in a sealed container in the refrigerator.

tahini meltaways

· ·

I made a peanut butter meltaway one holiday season, and the next spring, Alexis took the basic idea and swapped in tahini and the world went nuts, the cheering from the stands is still ringing in all our ears. No joke, this is pretty much everyone's favorite confection—staff, customers, crushes, the kind of thing that when you break up with your girlfriend and they stop coming by the shop what really gives you a secret mean thrill is knowing how much they'll miss those meltaways. It's one of the most savory sweets we make, and for sure the two are related. These are also shockingly easy to make. There is no downside to Tahini Meltaways. No thermometer needed; they're one of the fastest recipes in this book.

We buy 5-gallon buckets of this amazing tahini made by the folks at Soom, who source premium single-origin sesame seeds and roast them carefully. If you use regular supermarket tahini, these will be just fine, but premium tahini is a world away, creamier and tahini-er in wondrous ways.

This recipe makes one layer of white chocolate and a layer of milk chocolate meltaway, which are layered on each other and chopped into bite-size pieces. You are more than welcome to make only one layer of either variety, particularly because good vegan white chocolate can be hard to come by. Our house vegan milk chocolate is just a blend of our house-made white chocolate and dark chocolate. You can mix it yourself as we do, or you can use any brand of good vegan milk chocolate you can find instead of the white and dark chocolates.

Makes 32 meltaways

Milk chocolate meltaway

¼ cup/50 g coconut oil

Heaping ¼ cup/71 g tahini

½ teaspoon/2 g sea salt

½ teaspoon/3 g toasted sesame oil

⅓ cup/67 g dark chocolate, finely chopped

1 cup/146 g vegan white chocolate, finely chopped

White chocolate meltaway

¼ cup/50 g coconut oil

Heaping ¼ cup/71 g tahini

¼ teaspoon/2 g sea salt

½ teaspoon/3 g toasted sesame oil

1¼ cups/213 g vegan white chocolate, finely chopped

1 pound chocolate, for dipping (optional)

Optional garnish: toasted sesame seeds and/or sea salt

1. Line an 8 by 4-inch loaf pan or silicone pan with parchment paper on all sides. Be sure the parchment lines the sides of the pan. Wet the underside of the parchment before fitting it to the pan if it's being curly and uncooperative.
2. Prepare the milk chocolate meltaway layer: Melt the coconut oil in a 2-quart pot over very low heat, then whisk in the tahini, salt, and sesame oil until incorporated. Whisk in the dark and white chocolate over very low heat or off the heat, depending on how fluid the mixture is.
3. When completely emulsified, pour into the prepared pan and refrigerate until completely solid, 2 hours or so.
4. Prepare the white chocolate meltaway layer: Don't start this layer until the first layer is at least slightly solid, about 30 minutes. For best results, you want to pour the top layer onto the bottom while the bottom layer is soft enough that the two layers fuse together nicely, but not so soft that they collapse into each other and you lose layer definition.
5. Rinse out the same pan you used for the milk chocolate layer, and melt the coconut oil in it over very low heat, then whisk in the tahini, salt, and sesame oil until incorporated. Whisk in the white chocolate over very low heat or off the heat, depending on how fluid the mixture is.
6. When completely emulsified, pour into prepared pan over the first layer. Refrigerate until completely solid.
7. For best results, cut when the mixture is at room temperature. Cut into four by eight rows, for a total of thirty-two 1-inch-square pieces. Serve as is, or temper your dipping chocolate (see page 17), and dip the meltaways into it, using a dipping fork, regular fork, or your fingers. Garnish with toasted sesame seeds and/or sea salt.
8. The meltaways store beautifully in a tightly covered container in the refrigerator for up to 1 month.

(recipe photo shown on cover)

acknowledgments

Thank you, Maresa Volante, for being a brilliant business partner and best friend, and for putting up with over ten years of my insane venting, ranting, plotting, and planning. Thanks for keeping my secrets. Here's to another couple decades of scheming.

Thank you, Elizabeth Pachaud, for being a crisis-friend and an equally competent best friend in noncrisis times. I love you deeply and madly, you are my family.

Thank you, Than Luu, for two decades of TF, all the unbelievable outfits, the endless deep love, support, pep talks, continually foiled attempts to get me high, SexSecrets, etc., etc., etc.

Thank you, Juan Luis Carrera and Molly Rausch Carrera, for (1) Mr. F., (2) your decades of friendship, and (3) giving me an anchor in the form of the most beautiful place I've ever been lucky enough to call home.

Thank you, Mike McGregor, for your love of fruit and life, your strength, and deeply fun spirit.

Thank you, Rachel Jordan, Lyndsey Cooper, and Dot Dulgarian for being the beating heart of Commissary! and always anchoring our world in love, softness, and deep friendship.

Thank you especially to Rachel Jordan, for your unbelievable work ethic which matches my own so closely, your sense of humor, and your friendship.

Thank you, Kate Larson, Alexis Tellefsen, Jenn Varon, and Shelly Karan, for being the beating heart of Lagusta's Luscious, for running a chocolate empire, bringing my insane ideas down to earth, and teaching me so much about trust, kindness, and what we can accomplish together.

Thank you, Veronica Timan, for being the beating heart of Confectionery!, an anchor of sweetness in a dirty city, someone I've been honored to be able to watch grow up, and a constant inspiration on a million levels (eyebrow, style, heartfeltness, etc., ad infinitum).

Thank you to the music of (and person of) Mary Lattimore, which became a guidepost for focusing my brain and a signal to step out of running three businesses and into the world of writing this book.

Thank you, MutualMuse Brooks Headley, for responding to anguished book-stressed two a.m. texts and encouraging me to weave weirdness into the threads of the book so hugely that no amount of editing could unweird it.

Thank you, Mark Portier, for friendship, cheerleading, listening, and always being in my corner.

Thank you to my sweet brother, Leonard Yearwood—Len! I love you. If you have to only have one family member on earth, I'm endlessly glad it's you.

Thank you, Timothy Edward Rogers, Rafi Rogers, and Nina Sol Rogers, for being the fun, fascinating people you are. I'm so happy to be in your lives.

Thank you, Kara Davis, for the title of this book and, along with Korn, building a friendship I cherish.

Thank you, Jacob Jon Minor Feinberg-Pyne, for twenty unbelievable years of teaching each other how to be human beings, and how to eat. I'm grateful for your good appetite.

Thank you, Christy Hall (and Eleanor and Petra Blueberry Wassum), for being an endlessly inspiring force for good + best doppelgänger for the past two-plus decades. Here's to our roots: nonviolent direct action.

Thank you to my ex-sister-out-law Pohanna Pyne-Feinberg. Knowing you the past twenty+ years has enriched my life so much.

Sincere, heartfelt, bottomless thanks to my agent Meg Thompson (I really admire how you pull off those hoop earrings!), and Renée Sedliar, a supremely lovely and patient editor whose cuts were vital and compassionate. Thank you, Iris Bass, for such thorough copyedits. Thank you, Tabitha Lahr, for an interior design that matches the anarchy of our shop, and Kerry Rubenstein, for a kickass cover.

Thank you, Ericka Wadleigh, for an amazing author photo.

Thank you, Anne Conger and Gonzales the turtle; Jess Davis and James David Saul, for wasp nests and friendship; and Chloe Wilkinson for the loan of your leg and hands.

Thank you to my delightfully menschy exshrink, Peter Kaplan, for continually reminding me that the world won't end if I'm not perfect, even though truthfully I did pay you to say it, but still.

Thank you to the NYC Public Library system, various coffee shops I do not own, Pakt, the window seat at Commissary! which I hogged for way too long, Jar'd wine pub, Laura Burhenn's Echo Park dreamhouse, fancy hotel lobbies around Manhattan and Brooklyn, and other secret spaces where most of this book was written, on stolen time from three needy businesses.

Thank you to the Lagusta's Luscious, Confectionery!, and Commissary! crews for expertly running the businesses and allowing me to shut off my phone on Thursdays so my brain could stretch out enough to get these words out.

Thank you to the following amazing recipe testers, those scattered around the world and those at Lagusta's Luscious: Amara Dieter, Sam Hemphill, Shelly Karan, Kate Larson, Holly Manz, Jenna McDavid, Erika Olver, Elizabeth Pachaud, Jill Pucciarelli, Randy Putnam, Vidya Ramachandran, Eliza Sloane, Alexis Tellefsen, Jasmine Towers, Jenn Varon.

Love

I love you and want to say your name here:

Carol Adams, Erin Casteel, Barbara Chapman, Harriet Choice, Jen Constantine, Ruby Des Jardins, Aaron Di Orio, Moira Dwyer, Nicole Georges, Anandhi Lion Feinberg, Deena Feinberg-Pyne, Mika Feinberg, River Azul Feinberg Pyne Vial, Warunee Feinberg, Noel Furie, Ken Greene, Justin Goellner, Benjamin Page Kellogg, Doug Muller, Tara Pelletier, Natalie Pitchford-Levy, Rachelle Pyne, Randy and Lacey Putnam, Selma Miriam, Katy O'Brien, Maya Projansky, Jasmine Redfern, Dustin Rhodes, John Smylie, Megan and Sarah Snow, Trippy Thompson, Judy Voigt.

Kate's Fizz (page 179)

index
